Devil's Advocates

DEVIL'S ADVOCATES is a series of books devoted to exploring the classics of horror cinema. Contributors to the series come from the fields of teaching, academia, journalism and fiction, but all have one thing in common: a passion for the horror film and a desire to share it with the widest possible audience.

'The admirable Devil's Advocates series is not only essential – and fun – reading for the serious horror fan but should be set texts on any genre course.'
Dr Ian Hunter, Reader in Film Studies, De Montfort University, Leicester

'Auteur Publishing's new Devil's Advocates critiques on individual titles... offer bracingly fresh perspectives from passionate writers. The series will perfectly complement the BFI archive volumes.' **Christopher Fowler,** *Independent on Sunday*

'Devil's Advocates has proven itself more than capable of producing impassioned, intelligent analyses of genre cinema... quickly becoming the go-to guys for intelligent, easily digestible film criticism.' *Horror Talk.com*

'Auteur Publishing continue the good work of giving serious critical attention to significant horror films.' *Black Static*

 DevilsAdvocatesbooks

DevilsAdBooks

Also available in this series

A Girl Walks Home Alone at Night Farshid Kazemi
Black Sunday Martyn Conterio
The Blair Witch Project Peter Turner
Blood and Black Lace Roberto Curti
The Blood on Satan's Claw David Evans-Powell
Candyman Jon Towlson
Cannibal Holocaust Calum Waddell
Cape Fear Rob Daniel
Carrie Neil Mitchell
The Company of Wolves James Gracey
The Conjuring Kevin J. Wetmore Jr.
Creepshow Simon Brown
Cruising Eugenio Ercolani & Marcus Stiglegger
The Curse of Frankenstein Marcus K. Harmes
Daughters of Darkness Kat Ellinger
Dawn of the Dead Jon Towlson
Dead of Night Jez Conolly & David Bates
The Descent James Marriot
The Devils Darren Arnold
Don't Look Now Jessica Gildersleeve
The Evil Dead Lloyd Haynes
The Fly Emma Westwood
Frenzy Ian Cooper
Halloween Murray Leeder
House of Usher Evert Jan van Leeuwen
In the Mouth of Madness Michael Blyth
IT Chapters One and Two Alissa Burger

It Follows Joshua Grimm
Ju-on The Grudge Marisa Hayes
Let the Right One In Anne Billson
M Samm Deighan
Macbeth Rebekah Owens
The Mummy Doris V. Sutherland
Nosferatu Cristina Massaccesi
The Omen Adrian Schober
Peeping Tom Kiri Bloom Walden
Possession Alison Taylor
Re-Animator Eddie Falvey
Repulsion Jeremy Carr
Saw Benjamin Poole
Scream Steven West
The Shining Laura Mee
Shivers Luke Aspell
The Silence of the Lambs Barry Forshaw
Suspiria Alexandra Heller-Nicholas
The Texas Chain Saw Massacre James Rose
The Thing Jez Conolly
Trouble Every Day Kate Robertson
Twin Peaks: Fire Walk With Me Lindsay Hallam
Witchfinder General Ian Cooper

Forthcoming

The Cabin in the Woods Susanne Kord
The Craft Miranda Corcoran
Poltergeist Rob McLaughlin

Devil's Advocates

Pet Sematary

Shellie McMurdo

First published in 2023 by
Auteur, an imprint of
Liverpool University Press,
4 Cambridge Street,
Liverpool
L69 7ZU

This paperback edition published 2025

Series design: Nikki Hamlett at Cassels Design
Set by Carnegie Book Production, Lancaster

All rights reserved. No part of this publication may be reproduced in any material form (including photocopying or storing in any medium by electronic means and whether or not transiently or incidentally to some other use of this publication) without the permission of the copyright owner.

British Library Cataloguing-in-Publication Data
A catalogue record for this book is available from the British Library
ISBN hardback: 978-1-80207-718-6
ISBN paperback: 978-1-83624-396-0
ISBN PDF: 978-1-80207-900-5

Contents

Figures vii

Introduction: 'Come on doc, we've got places to go' 1

Chapter 1: 'You'll have all the grief you can stand and more': the centrality of grief in *Pet Sematary* 7

Chapter 2: 'Couldn't plant anything here but corpses anyway': contextualising *Pet Sematary* 21

Chapter 3: 'The ground is sour': analysing *Pet Sematary* 39

Chapter 4: 'A place where the dead speak': authorship and the production of *Pet Sematary* 61

Chapter 5: 'Sometimes dead is better' (?): revisiting and remaking Stephen King and *Pet Sematary* 81

Legacy and conclusion: 'Here's to your bones' 99

Bibliography 103

Acknowledgements

I am incredibly thankful for the support of a large number of people, without whom the completion of this work would not have been possible. First of all, enormous thanks are due to John Atkinson, who took a chance on me at an early stage in my career. John's encouragement, support, and advice (and patience with panicked emails) on both this and other ventures has been unwavering and much appreciated. My thanks go too to Stacey Abbott who has been a great mentor and a great friend, and Simon Brown, whose work on Stephen King adaptations has been indispensable (and also for very kind words on this book!). Special thanks go also to Rebecca Janicker who reached out to me early in this project and helped immensely. I guess it would be weird to not thank Stephen King – who wrote the Creed family into this world, and Mary Lambert – who gave them life on screen.

Thanks as always go to my Monster Squad – Stella Gaynor, Craig Mann, Laura Mee, and Tom Watson – who I hope know the place that they hold in my regard and in my heart. They managed to cheer me up on every down day, are the most supportive of peers, and are just general all-around good folks. Especially grateful thanks are owed to Laura Mee in particular, who was my constant companion through the frankly terrifying final weeks of writing this book.

Endless thanks go to my mum, Patricia, who I think knew that I was secretly watching horror films when I was way too young for them, and her dog, Juno, who kept me entertained during long days of writing. Of course, eternal thanks are owed to my husband Colin, who has had to sit through Louis Creed's descent into madness so many times he probably knows each line, and who is often distraught when he accidentally finds himself analysing a film.

This book is dedicated to my husband – without who I would surely crumble – and my own dog, Hemingway, who has kept me company through both the writing of this book, and all my filmic visits to Ludlow, Maine.

Figures

Figure 1. The scene that launched thousands of my nightmares 2

Figure 2. How does one know if a cat "begins" to act viciously? 5

Figure 3. 'If it doesn't work [...] I'll just put him back to sleep': Louis is grimly
determined to resurrect Gage 10

Figure 4. Gage returns 11

Figure 5. A reanimated Rachel's injuries, sustained at the hands of her child 17

Figure 6. 'Instant junk'/horror classic *The Thing* 25

Figure 7. From top left, the trailers for *Carrie*, *The Dead Zone*, *Maximum Overdrive*,
and *Silver Bullet* 31

Figure 8. Timmy Baterman's zombie like appearance 35

Figure 9. The recurring outfit throughout *Pet Sematary* 42

Figure 10. Rachel's childhood home is filled with photographic memories 43

Figure 11. Clear blue skies and promises of friendship 45

Figure 12. Pastoral scenes in Ludlow, Maine 46

Figure 13. Louis fails to catch Gage 47

Figure 14. Louis's fragile hold on sanity is slipping fast 51

Figure 15. The burial ground 55

Figure 16. Jud's house is reclaimed by the land 56

Figure 17. Always look under the bed for scalpel wielding toddlers 75

Figure 18. The expressionistic influence within *Pet Sematary* 76

Figure 19. *Pet Sematary 2* ties itself visually to the original film 84

Figure 20. Dead but together in *Pet Sematary* 2019...................96

Figure 21. One last caress....................101

Introduction: 'Come on doc, we've got places to go'

For any horror fan growing up in the late 1990s, the Treehouse of Horror episodes of the long-running animated sitcom *The Simpsons* (Fox, 1989–) were a fun little treat. My own clandestine horror viewing – which was mostly through fuzzy VHS copies of copies and watching late night television with the sound on low while my parents slept – was supplemented by these kid-friendly Halloween offerings. These sat alongside reruns of *Eerie, Indiana* (NBC, 1991–1992), various Point Horror books, and *The Monster Squad* (Fred Dekker, 1987) as my childhood gateway drugs to the horror genre.

In "Treehouse of Horror III" (S04 E05), Bart Simpson takes his sister Lisa to Springfield's pet cemetery and attempts to perform a ritual to bring Lisa's much-loved cat, Snowball I, back to life. Unfortunately, he messes up the ritual and calls forth hundreds of zombies from the adjacent human cemetery, which then terrorise the neighbourhood. A rerun of "Treehouse of Horror III" was not my first entanglement with *Pet Sematary*, however. I was the ripe age of seven or eight when I ran screaming from the room as Victor Pascow sat up, head oozing brain matter, to deliver his cryptic warning about sour ground to Louis Creed (see Figure 1). Although my stamina for gore would improve over the subsequent years, *Pet Sematary* had such an impact on me that it would be at least a decade before I dared to revisit the film. As a horror scholar, I always knew I would find myself back in the "Sematary" at some point and I do not recount my formative experiences with the film to somehow qualify my horror credentials, or to justify why I consider it to be worthy of analysis. It is more to express how – at least for me – *Pet Sematary* is a film that stays with you, long after it cuts to black, and The Ramones play out.

Most scholarship on *Pet Sematary* overarchingly focuses on the novel, and tends strongly towards housing the story within the Gothic literary tradition. The film itself is often absent from considerations of 1980s North American horror cinema, and from wider horror scholarship in general. For example, in an account detailing the ways in which the concept of the American Dream is presented in a variety of films released in 1989, Jennifer Holt (2007) mentions a sole horror film, *Parents* (Bob Balaban, 1989) but ignores *Pet Sematary*. This is despite the fact that her chapter focuses on the year of *Pet Sematary*'s release, that *Pet Sematary* was the highest grossing horror film that year, and that – as I will argue – it is a narrative that interrogates and dismantles ideas around the American Dream brutally. Similarly, Jessica Balanzalegui (2018) dedicates a whole section of *The Uncanny Child in Transnational Cinema: Ghosts of Futurity at the Turn of the Twenty-First Century* to American horror films and, within that section, includes a chapter on the 1980s specifically; but *Pet Sematary* does not warrant a mention. Additionally, although it receives a citation as a horror film directed by a woman in Adam Lowenstein's consideration of what he terms 'feminine horror' (2015: 483), *Pet Sematary* is only noted, not analysed. It is fair to say then that there have been very few considerations of *Pet Sematary* – the film – of any significant length.[1] This book stands therefore as a corrective, and will provide a holistic analysis – textual, contextual, and industrial – of the film, which has thus far been critically neglected, in order to properly situate it as an important entry into the history of horror cinema.

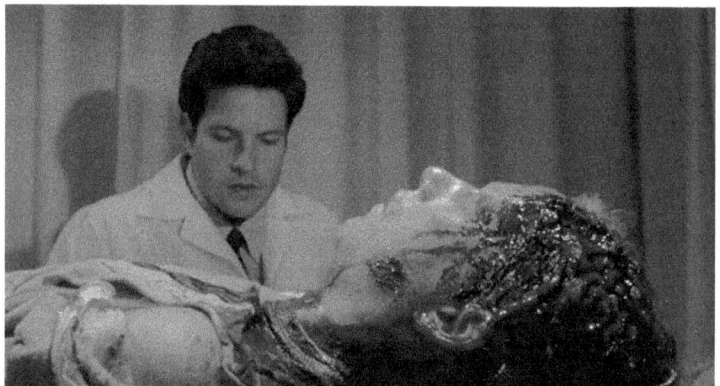

Figure 1. The scene that launched thousands of my nightmares

Pet Sematary is a particularly interesting Stephen King adaptation due to the author's presence as its screenwriter and on set during the production. Indeed, its creation was made possible only under a list of conditions created by King. In contrast to the animosity King reportedly felt for the adaptation of *The Shining* (Stanley Kubrick, 1980) at the start of the decade, the collaborative and seemingly harmonious relationship between King and Mary Lambert, the director of *Pet Sematary*, is noteworthy. Simon Brown has argued that accounts of King adaptations will often tie films together thematically, with little attention being paid to their contextual and industrial differences such as budget, director, studio, or indeed how they have emerged at different points in cinematic horror history (2018: 7). A further aim of this book therefore is to properly situate *Pet Sematary* within the context of 1980s North American horror cinema, with a consideration of the level of unprecedented visibility the genre gained in that decade, and how that visibility led to critical opprobrium and a lasting perception of 1980s horror as a tasteless and vapid period in genre history. Aiming to compliment accounts of 1980s horror that primarily explore the centrality of the slasher subgenre or the video nasties panic, this book will outline other varied ways in which the genre developed over the decade. Within these pages I will explore how *Pet Sematary* functioned in this context as a film that simultaneously adhered to genre expectations while departing from them, principally through its engagement with a nihilism more common to 1970s realist horror.

Although a nihilistic form of grief is certainly the central theme of *Pet Sematary*, to focus on this alone would be to do the film a disservice. Concepts such as the family and fatherhood as represented in the film, for example, were not only part of a wider trend in 1980s horror, but recurrent in Stephen King's work more broadly. Additionally, it would be remiss for a volume on *Pet Sematary* to not address the problematic presence of the "Indian Burial Ground" within the story. The analysis of the themes and conventions of the film you will find in this book will demonstrate their resonance in the ten-year period in between King's writing *Pet Sematary* and Mary Lambert's filmic version.

It may not have escaped the reader's attention that this book is part of a series that focuses on films considered to be the classics of the genre, and that it joins several entries in that series in focusing on a horror film directed by a woman. As such, in the pages that follow I dedicate a substantial amount of time to the relationship between women and horror cinema. Horror has traditionally been perceived as a male space, and this is due not only to a lack of attention afforded to women working within the genre historically, but wider perceptions regarding horror spectatorship. More recent horror media created by women has been enjoying a boom in visibility – as a following chapter will outline – but, as Alison Peirse states, 'Until we fully engage with historical materials, our understanding of women's contributions to genre cinema remains faulty and incomplete' (2020b: 14). This book joins a growing body of works – both journalistic and academic – that aim to revisit older films in order to call attention to and/or redress the gendered imbalance in our written horror histories.

This volume, then, charges *Pet Sematary* with several contributions to the horror genre. It is an important entry within the tradition of "grief horror"; it is a horror film that both adheres to and defies the generic conventions of its historical context; it is both engaged with and respondent to its time of creation; it changed the fortunes of the cinematic Stephen King "brand" on the cusp of a new decade; it is the highest grossing horror film directed by a woman in cinematic history; and it stands as a story that we keep returning to – as seen by the 1992 sequel, the 2019 remake, and a forthcoming prequel. *Pet Sematary*'s modern relevance and importance to genre history then, is manifold, and the film is primed for reconsideration and canonisation as a classic of horror cinema.

Synopsis

Pet Sematary centres on the Creed family, who have moved from Chicago, Illinois to Ludlow, Maine for a slower pace of life. As they arrive at their new home, we are quickly introduced to Louis Creed (Dale Midkiff), an MD who is about to begin a new job at the local university, his wife Rachel (Denise Crosby), their young daughter Ellie (Blaze Berdahl/Beau Berdahl), and their toddler son Gage (Miko Hughes). While Louis and Rachel tend to Ellie, who has fallen from a tyre swing in the front garden, Gage wanders towards the road and perilously close to a large truck. Gage is quickly snatched out of the road by Jud Crandall (Fred Gwynne) who introduces himself to the Creeds as their new neighbour.

Louis strikes up a friendship with Jud, who is a lifelong Ludlow resident, and it is through Jud that the Creeds are introduced to the pet cemetery – misspelled "Pet Sematary" by the local children that created it – which is situated behind their property. Despite Jud's attempts to allay her fears about the cemetery, Ellie becomes upset after visiting it, realising that one day her cat, Church, will die. In an attempt to placate his daughter, and his wife – who has an aversion to discussing death – Louis agrees to get Church neutered in the hope that it will stop him straying too far from the house and takes the cat to the vet on the way to his first day as the university doctor.

Louis's first day – at the risk of massive understatement – does not go well. A student named Victor Pascow (Brad Greenquist) is hit by a truck while jogging on campus and suffers fatal injuries, dying in Louis's office. Alone with the body, Louis is aghast when Victor suddenly returns to life and vows to visit Louis before then collapsing back into death. That night, as promised, Pascow returns to Louis as he lies in bed and leads him to the pet cemetery. Once there, Pascow warns that Louis should not 'go on to the place where the dead walk', which, he suggests with a pointed finger, lies beyond the wall of dead branches and fallen trees in the cemetery. Upon waking the next morning, Louis's muddied feet suggest that Pascow's visitation was not a mere nightmare.

Some time later, while Rachel, Ellie, and Gage spend Thanksgiving with Rachel's parents back in Chicago, Church is killed in the road. Jud and Louis travel to the pet cemetery to bury the cat, but Jud leads Louis beyond the deadfall and, despite Pascow's warning, Louis follows. The two men travel to what Jud describes as an ancient burial ground, and he instructs Louis to 'bury his own' in the thin soil. The next day, Church returns to the Creed house. Seeking answers for this unnerving feline resurrection, Louis speaks with Jud, who explains that he brought his beloved dog back to life the same way when he was a boy, after being shown the power of the Micmac ground by a local man who had Native American heritage. Church is seemingly changed by his return from the dead and begins to act viciously (Figure 2).

Figure 2. How does one know if a cat "begins" to act viciously?

After their housekeeper, Missy Dandridge (Susan Bommaert), commits suicide, Rachel tries to explain the reason for her avoidance of the subjects of death and dying to Louis, and relays her traumatic childhood experience of the illness and death of her sister, Zelda (Andrew Hubatsek). Rachel is forced to confront death a short while later, however, when Gage is killed in the road after chasing a kite spool into the path of a truck during a family picnic. After Gage's funeral, Jud visits Louis as he suspects that the latter may be entertaining the idea of resurrecting Gage using the Micmac ground. Jud warns Louis away from this idea by telling him the story of Timmy Baterman (Peter Stader), a young man who was brought back from the dead to violent and tragic consequences. A few days later, Rachel and Ellie leave for Chicago while Louis remains in Maine and, despite the warnings of both Jud and Pascow, the latter of whom appears again to plead with Louis to rethink, he exhumes Gage's body. Ellie has a vivid nightmare in Chicago after which she claims a man named 'Paxcow' told her Louis was going to 'do something really bad' and an unnerved Rachel has a vision of her dead sister. Scared, Rachel leaves Ellie in Chicago and hurries back to Maine.

Having been buried in the ancient ground, Gage returns to the Creed home and steals a scalpel from Louis's bag as his father sleeps, before travelling to Jud's house across the road. Gage then taunts the older man before killing him. Rachel arrives back home and is lured to Jud's house, where she too is murdered by Gage. Upon waking, Louis notices small muddy footprints in the house and finds that his scalpel is missing. After receiving a menacing phone call from Gage, Louis travels across the road with syringes full of morphine, his intention being to put his resurrected son down. After killing Church with one of the syringes, Louis discovers the bodies of Jud and Rachel and, following a brief battle, he manages to inject Gage and kill him. Louis lights Jud's house on fire and leaves Gage's body to burn as he, now insane, carries Rachel to the Micmac ground. The film ends with a graphically injured and reanimated Rachel returning home to embrace Louis. As they kiss, Rachel grasps a knife and raises it. The screen cuts to black, and Louis screams.

NOTES

1. There are, of course, exceptions to this. The film has been covered in numerable aca-fan accounts, such as the particularly striking analysis carried out by Murphy (2017). Meanwhile, Jeffrey Weinstock (2008) discusses the connections between *Pet Sematary* and *Stand By Me* (Rob Reiner, 1986), and Tony Magistrale (2003) includes a chapter in *Hollywood's Stephen King* on father figures in a variety of films based on King works. Neither of these accounts focus on *Pet Sematary* alone, however.

Chapter 1: 'You'll have all the grief you can stand and more': the centrality of grief in *Pet Sematary*

Existing scholarly work on *Pet Sematary* tends to predominantly focus on the 1983 novel, and these previous academic interventions commonly centre on the ways in which *Pet Sematary* can be positioned within the Gothic tradition (see for example Pharr, 1987; Strengell, 2005; Armstrong, 2016 to name only a few). A variety of scholars have debated where King's work falls in terms of this literary history. John Sears, for example, has noted that while the Gothic is mobilised in a variety of ways within King's oeuvre, his work can be situated as a continuation of the American Gothic tradition specifically (2011: 158). Rebecca Janicker is more precise still, and argues that, particularly in the case of *Pet Sematary*, 'the shadow of the Puritan inheritance and a lingering dread of the land itself' (2007: np) suggests that King's work is an example of a regionalist New England Gothic tale. Meanwhile, other scholars have compared King's narratives to older Gothic stories and, in doing so, have tied him to this genre through association.

A detailed analysis of all the ways in which *Pet Sematary* has been said to adhere to, engage with, and reframe the Gothic would likely necessitate a book of its own. Therefore, I will limit my discussion here to some of the more widely known conventions of the Gothic in relation to *Pet Sematary* in order to outline this preoccupation in previous work and some of its potential limitations. This chapter will, using a basis in trauma studies, instead put forward an argument for consideration of *Pet Sematary* as part of the ongoing history of what I will tentatively call "grief horror" and will focus on the cyclical nature of familial trauma as key to the story. Moreover, I seek to recentre *Pet Sematary* as, first and foremost, a *horror* – rather than a Gothic – film.

'I know you don't approve of the subject': before we begin, a note on the gothic and *Pet Sematary*

The most evident link between the Gothic and *Pet Sematary* is often argued to be its narrative similarities to older Gothic stories. This can be seen in particular in comparisons to the W. W. Jacobs short story, *The Monkey's Paw* (1902), in which a mother and father, Mr and Mrs White, come into possession of a magical monkey's paw, which grants them three wishes. Not wanting to be greedy, Mr and Mrs White wish for the exact amount of their final mortgage payment. Shortly afterwards, their son, Herbert, is killed in an accident while at work. The bereavement payment Herbert's company gives the Whites is the exact amount they wished for. Mrs White, driven mad with grief, insists on using the second wish to resurrect Herbert. Mr White, despite having a premonition of how their son will return to them horribly mangled by the accident, obeys his wife. A few hours later, there is a knock at the door and Mr White, terrified of the possibility of the return of a creature who bears no resemblance to his son, uses the last wish to undo the previous one. The story ends with Mrs White flinging open the door and sobbing when she finds no one there. The resemblance between *Pet Sematary* and *The Monkey's Paw* is clear. Both narratives feature a much-loved son who is returned from the dead and makes his way home, the monkey's paw – which in the story originates from India – possesses an unknown and markedly "foreign" magical power, much like the Micmac burial ground of *Pet Sematary* and, at a stretch, we can transpose the three wishes in the older story to the three resurrections attempted by Louis: Church, Gage, and Rachel. More broadly in terms of antecedents, it is also possible to compare King's works to his predecessors within New England Gothic literary history such as H. P. Lovecraft and Shirley Jackson, with a particular tonal likeness being present within the opening lines of Jackson's *The Haunting of Hill House* (1959) and the paragraph that begins the second half of *Pet Sematary*.[1]

Particular attention too has been drawn to the apparent similitude between *Pet Sematary* and a work that belongs to what Kamilla Elliott terms the 'triptych' of the Gothic canon (2007: 223): Mary Shelley's *Frankenstein* (1818). The desperate need of Louis Creed to resurrect his son has been compared numerous times to the single-minded ambitions of Victor Frankenstein to conquer death and give life to non-living matter (see Schuman, 1987; Alegre, 2001; Janicker, 2007; Dymond, 2013; Burger, 2016). Lester Freidman and Alison Kavey have, for example, positioned *Pet Sematary* as a 'translation' of *Frankenstein*, with the most striking connection being that both Victor Frankenstein and Louis Creed are rational men of science and medicine but, despite this, they 'cannot withstand a Faustian temptation to fulfil their most ardent desires, and they succumb to the darkness by choosing their desires over their intellect' (2016: 180). Elsewhere, Mary Ferguson Pharr has argued that *Pet Sematary* 'amplif[ies] the cultural echo', Shelley's novel set in motion (1987: 120).

If one cared to stress this connection between the two texts, they could also cite the explicit reference to the cinematic history of *Frankenstein* within *Pet Sematary* to tie it closer to that 'cultural echo' of Shelley's tale. This reference occurs during a flashback scene after Gage's death, which accompanies Jud's cautionary tale of Timmy Baterman, who died in World War Two and was subsequently resurrected using the Micmac burial ground by his father, Bill (Chuck Courtney). Jud recounts to Louis how a group of men, including himself, took it upon themselves to correct this "abomination" by setting the Baterman house on fire while Timmy and his father were in it. Timmy grabs Bill and pulls him further into the burning house while shouting 'Love dead, hate living', a line previously uttered by Frankenstein's Monster to Doctor Pretorius in *The Bride of Frankenstein* (James Whale, 1935). This line is only present in the filmic *Pet Sematary*, however, and absent in the source novel.

While, as in *Frankenstein*, *Pet Sematary*'s narrative circles around the line between life and death and the wilful crossing of that line by a doctor, I would respectfully argue that, while superficially similar, these stories possess key differences. Victor Frankenstein is driven by ego and an ambition to create life from dead matter in the name of science, procuring his raw materials by robbing graves. After giving his monster life, Frankenstein is repulsed by his creation and then terrorised by it. Louis Creed, however, is characterised as a firmly rational man who has no interest in crossing the boundary between life and death until his son is killed. It is true that one could argue that Louis's curiosity regarding this boundary – and the beginning of his journey into madness – starts with the resurrection of Church. This reading is flawed, however, as the cat dies and is buried in the Micmac ground before Louis fully realises the power that resides there. During the scenes detailing Church's burial and return, Louis is in turn incredulous and unsure. When Jud tells Louis they are going beyond the pet cemetery and over the deadfall, Louis – perhaps half remembering his warning from Pascow a few nights previous – initially balks but then follows Jud somewhat reluctantly. Although Jud mentions the history of the burial ground as they arrive, he does not go into detail as to the reasons he has brought Louis there, driving Louis to ask 'Why for God's sake? I said "Why?" Jud!'. It is only once the men are back at the Creed house and Jud prompts a flashback to Pascow's death by stating that 'the soil of a man's heart is stonier' – a line previously spoken by Pascow as he died – that Louis pales, seemingly realising for the first time that he has crossed a dangerous boundary. The following day Louis is still clinging to rationality, examining the resurrected Church before speaking with Jud about the possibility that he buried the cat alive. It is only after this that Jud then explains the power of the Micmac ground more thoroughly and Louis believes wholeheartedly that Church has returned from the dead. Therefore, I argue, that it is only in the days following Gage's death – after the return of Church, the explanation from Jud and later in the film, Jud's retelling of the story of Timmy Baterman – that Louis fully understands what he is undertaking, recognises the boundary he is crossing, and possesses full and lucid intention to return life to the dead (see Figure 3), making him a markedly different character than Victor Frankenstein.[2] Furthermore, there is a stark emotional difference between Frankenstein's reanimation of the dead flesh of people previously unknown to him, and Creed's hope of returning life to his own dead child. I am inclined therefore to agree with Jesse Nash's argument that 'If King is rewriting *Frankenstein*, he is rewriting it from a vastly different personal, cultural, and historical perspective [...] *Frankenstein* and *Pet Sematary* no longer share the same genre' (1997: 152).

Figure 3. 'If it doesn't work [...] I'll just put him back to sleep'. Louis is grimly determined to resurrect Gage

False similarities between the two stories are also noted by Mark Browning, who argues that despite attempts to compare several adaptations of King's works, including *The Lawnmower Man* (Brett Leonard, 1992) and *Firestarter* (Mark L. Lester, 1984), to *Frankenstein*, there is 'no mad scientist […] and no visible act of creation', and that rather than being scientifically assembled in a laboratory, 'the reanimated corpses simply appear' within *Pet Sematary* (2009: 12).

In addition to comparisons to *Frankenstein* specifically, it is quite easy to find other examples of conventions common to the Gothic within *Pet Sematary* that perhaps explain the desire to position it as part of this tradition. Rachel's sister, Zelda, who was – as Rachel puts it – kept 'in the back bedroom like a dirty secret', can stand in for the motif of the madwoman in the attic, for instance, and the resurrected Church, Gage, and Rachel are the living dead, the presence of which has been noted as one of the key thematic identifiers of the Gothic (Bell, 2013). Likewise, the presence of doubles or doppelgangers within the Gothic (Hopkins, 2005: xi–xii) can be seen in *Pet Sematary* not only through the evil revenants that loved ones return as but also through the two cemeteries at the heart of the narrative acting as binary opposites to one another. We can also read Gage's return from the dead specifically as an example of the return of the repressed (Castricano, 2001) (Figure 4), a convention cited as central to the Gothic narrative (Martin and Savoy, 1998), and through which *Pet Sematary* 'expresses a series of familiar Gothic concerns around the trope of resurrection' (Sears, 2011: 198).

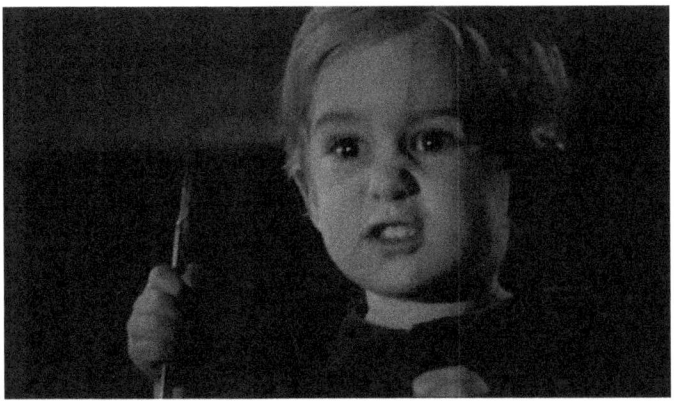

Figure 4. Gage returns

There is a danger here, however, of ignoring cultural and contextual specificity. Although I am not suggesting that there is anything necessarily "wrong" with reading *Pet Sematary* as Gothic and have indeed pointed towards several works in which this is a productive reading strategy, I wish to highlight the potential peril of unproductively homogenising texts under the banner of "Gothic" in order to neatly categorise them. As Xavier Aldana Reyes cautions, even though a film such as *Alien* (Ridley Scott, 1979) possesses Gothic traits such as a reliance on tension and obscurement of the monster, 'To refer to *Alien* as a Gothic film on the grounds that it plays like a haunted house story in space entails a rethinking of the Gothic that may stretch the term to the point where it becomes so broad as to lose all sense of specificity' (2020: 9). As such, there is a critical need to move beyond the tendency of trope-spotting for the purpose of tying a text to a particular literary tradition. There is also a parallel requirement to move away from the 'Gothicising' of texts, where vaguely affiliated notions are used to house a text within the Gothic – seemingly for the purpose of claiming it as belonging to that heritage – and instead a move towards rooting these analyses on more specific cultural and contextual foundations. In other words, this need to 'move beyond the identification of individual and disparate Gothic traits' (Reyes, 2020: 10) is essential, 'if the various darknesses and secrets are to be more than tropes' (Martin and Savoy, 1998: xi). Therefore, although we can comfortably position *Pet Sematary* as an example of the more specific New England Gothic tradition (as is done productively by Savoy, 1988; Janicker, 2007; and Sears, 2011 among others), we must also recognise the historical specificity of the story, being a novel published in 1983, and a film released in 1989. Accordingly, even though Chapter Three of this book will touch upon the destruction of the family unit, for example, which is widely considered to be a Gothic concern, this is done with a firm grounding in and with reference to the cultural milieu that *Pet Sematary* was conceived, published, and adapted within. Indeed, although it can be argued that *Pet Sematary* clearly engages with the Gothic, I maintain that it does not need to be couched within this specific tradition in order to appreciate its complexity or its legacy within popular culture. What is needed perhaps is a blended approach that accepts and recognises the inherently Gothic features of the text, while situating it firmly as an adaptation of a popular Stephen King book and as a cinematic product of the 1980s, with less attention being paid to a classical literary tradition, but more to popular culture itself, and how it 'appropriates, reworks, and re-presents' older stories and myths (Nash, 1997: 151).

An obligation to claim that *Pet Sematary* is immovably and solely Gothic may also be part of a wider attempt to reclaim King from the comparatively disreputable genre of horror fiction. Early disregard of King's work by literary critics seems to have been predicated around his status as a popular *horror* writer who, as Gary Hoppenstand and Ray B. Browne recall, was discounted as trite and unoriginal even during the 1980s peak of his literary success (1987: 2). Similarly, even after Stephen King received the prestigious Medal for Distinguished Contribution to American Letters prize from The National Book Awards, Harold Bloom observed that 'I've described King in the past as a writer of penny dreadfuls, but perhaps even that is too kind. He shares nothing with Edgar Allan Poe. What he is is an immensely inadequate writer on a sentence-by-sentence, paragraph-by-paragraph, book-by-book basis' (Bloom, 2003). Even in otherwise complimentary accounts, unfavourable comparisons between King and the "masters" of Gothic fiction are often foregrounded. For example, Mary Ferguson Pharr argues that King is 'Almost entirely derivative, [his] popular culture genius lies in his ability to redesign standard Gothic lore, to interpret rather than to originate', before noting that 'King is no Shelley' (1987: 115), whose writing – in comparison – is 'more important than anything [King] has yet produced' (1987: 120). The seemingly adversarial binary between Gothic and horror fiction can be traced back at least as far as to Ann Radcliffe's discussion of "terror" versus "horror", framed by Radcliffe as 'opposite', because 'the first expands the soul and awakens the faculties to a high degree of life; the other contracts, freezes and nearly annihilates them', before she notes that horror cannot ever be a source of the sublime (1826: 151). In other words, and as Devendra Varma skilfully explains, 'the difference between Terror and Horror is the difference between awful apprehension and sickening realization: between the smell of death and stumbling against a corpse' (1966: 130). The influence of the terror/horror binary has often seen horror – with its willingness to show gory spectacle – positioned as a poor relation to the more subtle and refined Gothic (which we can read as approximating "terror" in this binary classification), with the former often being reduced to a 'vulgar, exploitative version' of the latter (Hutchings, 1996: 89). As Xavier Aldana Reyes explains, this oppositional perspective runs the risk of 'denying horror (as it is understood in this taxonomy) its own potential value as more than a collection of gruesome moments' (2020: 9). In summary, I follow journalist Jason Bailey's statement that 'if anything should get to just be regular ol' horror, it's a film adaptation of an '80s Stephen King book' (Bailey, 2019). Therefore, it is the intention of the remainder of this chapter – and this book more broadly – to place *Pet Sematary* quite firmly within the horror genre, and as part of a history of horror films that have grappled with the subject of grief.

'You're thinking thoughts best not thought of': mourning and grief in *Pet Sematary*

It is not surprising, given that horror – perhaps more than any other genre – is preoccupied with death, that the theme of grief is recurrent in its history. Horror has long been used as a vehicle for exploring and expressing national grief and trauma, with volumes as *Shocking Representations: Historical Trauma, National Cinema, and the Modern Horror Film* (Lowenstein, 2005) and *The Wounds of Nations: Horror Cinema, Historical Trauma and National Identity* (Blake, 2008) engaging with this in detail. Although it is a more personal familial grief and the process of individual mourning that are the central themes that *Pet Sematary*'s narrative is organised around, it is possible to use trauma theory – which is concerned primarily with how the wounds, both metaphorical and literal, left by national trauma are represented in a nation's cultural products – as a framework through which to examine the film.

Following the critical success of films such as *Hereditary* (Ari Aster, 2018), there was a flurry of journalistic attention paid to how grief functions and is presented within the horror genre. Rafael Motamayor, for example, argues that the theme of grief is common in horror cinema because 'of how vulnerable we are at times of loss' (2018). Meanwhile, Guy Lodge of *The Guardian* proposes that horror cinema's ability to 'look death in the face and scream' (2018), makes it an excellent medium for representations of mourning. Additionally, several resonant and powerful essays have detailed personal accounts of the relationship between grief, mourning, the healing process, and the horror genre, and these should not be overlooked. Scout Tafoya, for example, writes on his own experience of the comforts that can be found in horror cinema, and how –

following the deaths of two of his friends – he desired to engage with the genre's ability 'to look squarely into the abyss of loss and puke back what it finds all over me' (Tafoya, 2019). Meanwhile, Eren Orbey highlights his use of horror as a coping mechanism following the murder of his father, and how he has 'continued searching for the worst I can witness on screen, testing myself with images of agony that seem crueller than my own' (Orbey, 2016).

Becky Millar and Jonny Lee have suggested that horror, through the use of antagonistic forces within its narratives, 'is effective at representing the disruption to one's core, taken-for-granted beliefs or "assumptive world" that is characteristic of grief' (2021: 171). This utilisation of the horror genre as a means to confront death and grief is encapsulated in Christine S. Davis and Jonathan L. Crane's proposal that audiences use the horror genre to tackle death head on, and that images of death and dying in the genre 'suture the gap between the cultural – political, social, economic, genetic, scientific, hegemonic – and the personal' (2015: 420). Horror then – as a genre that is 'very much engaged with, rather than estranged from, traumatic history' (Lowenstein, 2005:10) – can clearly be used as a way of working through personal trauma and grief.

It is important to note at this point that although a great number of horror films feature death, not all feature grief. Steve Jones (2021) has demonstrated that in the post-modern slasher films of the late 1990s and early 2000s for example, characters often display a distinct air of callous indifference to the deaths of their friends and acquaintances. There is a strand of films throughout horror history, though, that make grief a key element of their narrative. While several films have detailed the grief felt at the death of friends (*The Ritual* (David Bruckner, 2017)), parents (*The Final Girls* (Todd Strauss-Schulson, 2015)), siblings (*The Vigil* (Keith Thomas, 2020); *Personal Shopper* (Olivier Assayas, 2016)), whole immediate families (*Midsommar* (Ari Aster, 2019)) and romantic partners (*The Babadook* (Jennifer Kent, 2014); *The Night House* (David Bruckner, 2020); *An Unquiet Grave* (Terence Krey, 2020)), it is fair to say that the majority of grief horror films focus on the loss of children. Having historical antecedents in films such as *Don't Look Now* (Nicolas Roeg, 1973) and *The Changeling* (Peter Medak, 1980), among others, many post-millennial horror films including *The Descent* (Neil Marshall, 2005), *Lake Mungo* (Joel Anderson, 2008), *Antichrist* (Lars von Trier, 2009), *Lyle* (Stewart Thorndike, 2015), *The Invitation* (Karyn Kusama, 2015), *We Are Still Here* (Ted Geoghegan, 2015), *A Dark Song* (Liam Gavin,

2017), and the aforementioned *Hereditary*, all centre on the grief of mourning parent(s), which is, as Emma Wilson notes 'popularly reckoned as an ultimate horror' (2003: 157). Additionally, several films, such as *Wake Wood* (David Keating, 2009) and *The Other Side of the Door* (Johannes Roberts, 2016) feature parents who attempt to bring their children back from the dead, however briefly that may be for.[3]

Grief, and the fear of death, make up the foundational structure of *Pet Sematary*, with a narrative that is simultaneously horrific and heart-breaking. As Megan Nolan notes in her retrospective account of the novel, 'What makes *Pet Sematary* so uniquely awful is not an undead child – it's the [...] painfully precise portrait of grief, desperation, and madness' (2019), and as Sara Martin Alegre proposes, 'grief springing out of love is the real monster' (2001: 12) within the narrative. There is an inexorable quality to the grief and sadness in *Pet Sematary*, and the film maintains a sense of complete hopelessness that is quite unlike other King adaptations, as the next chapter will argue further.

Bryan Brown, in his study of what he terms the 'grief genre' (2009: 38) in contemporary American cinema, does not, unfortunately, detail the specific ways in which the horror genre engages with grief. He does, however, suggest that in the United States particularly, 'grief is treated as a hurdle that one must overcome – and done so quickly' (2009: 41). In relation to this, T. S. Kord has argued that the harmless pet cemetery, where generations of Ludlow's children have come to bury and mourn their pets, is implied in the film to be part of the "correct" grieving process (2016: 63). This can be seen too in Jud's aside to Ellie that the cemetery, in addition to being a place 'where the dead speak', is 'not a scary place, Ellie, it's a place of rest', and when he tells Louis after Church's burial that death is where 'the pain stops, and the good memories begin', thus positioning death and grieving as a natural process. Although Tony Magistrale asserts that 'Creed's compulsion to deliver the bodies of his son and wife to the cemetery is not adequately explained as a consequence of his guilt and grief' (1988: 11), I argue that it is precisely Louis Creed's grief, and his family's inability to process grief more generally, that leads to their downfall. Their mourning – Louis's in particular being mixed with guilt that he was not able to protect his son – crosses a boundary into a "deviant" form of grief.

Mourning shapes the Creed's interactions and beliefs in *Pet Sematary*, and the disastrous knock-on effect of inherited trauma and grief is at the heart of many actions and reactions within the narrative. For example, the parental neglect that Rachel suffered at the hands of her parents, who left her as an eight-year-old child to care for her seriously ill sister, results in Rachel's inability to deal with or even discuss death or grief.[4] This then perhaps influences Ellie's reaction after visiting the pet cemetery to the possibility that Church might one day die. The promise – or threat – of Ellie's potential emotional upset over the death of her cat then leads to Jud being inspired to take Louis to the Micmac burial ground. Without Jud doing this, Louis would not have known he could resurrect Gage. The destructive inheritance of unresolved trauma and repressed grief therefore is clear.

The conclusion of the film drives home the idea that familial trauma has a circular nature, that the Creeds are hopeless against this, and that a failure to grieve appropriately can only lead to ruin. In the final scene of the film, after burying his wife in the Micmac ground, Louis sits on the floor in the Creed family kitchen playing solitaire and, as the clock strikes midnight, Rachel returns home. We are first shown Rachel's hand as it creeps around the door, her fingernails broken and covered in blood, we then see her torn stockings and bloodied legs, one shoe missing as she limps into the kitchen. Louis stands to greet his wife and it is then that we bear witness to the horrific injuries Rachel sustained at the hands of her reanimated son (Figure 5).

Figure 5. A reanimated Rachel's injuries, sustained at the hands of her child

A portion of her face is missing, her eye socket leaking fluid as Louis leans to embrace and kiss her passionately. Unbeknownst to Louis, Rachel reaches for a kitchen knife that has been left on the table and, in slow motion, she raises it. The shot cuts to black as Louis screams. The monster is not vanquished and there is no happy ending for the Creeds. Instead, the theme that emerges forcefully at the close of the film is the end of any hope we may have had of the balance between good and evil being restored, and the complete annihilation of the family unit at the hands of grief. The real horror of *Pet Sematary* does not stem from the presence of the reanimated dead, from Pascow's night-time hauntings, or from the mutilation of Rachel and Jud at the hands of Gage, but more because it carefully invokes the American Dream only to cruelly dismember it – a key aspect of the film that I will explore further in Chapter Three. The death and destruction in *Pet Sematary*, as well as the grief, has an inevitable or fatalistic quality to it, and the film plays out as a series of worst-case scenarios in which Louis, in his scramble to escape the hole he has dug himself through guilt and grief, slips further and further into his own grave – bringing his family down with him.

Although comparisons between *Pet Sematary* and older Gothic tales – particularly *Frankenstein* – are common then, their similarities remain at a surface level, and there is a stark difference in terms of character motivation and the driving emotion behind their actions. This fixation on claiming *Pet Sematary* as Gothic also somewhat ignores several specificities of the film. This chapter has instead presented a counter reading of *Pet Sematary* as an example of the grief horror strand of the horror genre – a subset of films that is rapidly gaining more attention both in academia and more broadly. Although a future chapter will highlight other key themes of *Pet Sematary*, it is grief that is the central motivating emotion in the narrative, which stands as a cautionary tale about the potential dangers of unprocessed grief and refusing to engage with that which comes to us all.

Notes

1. Compare Jackson's 'No live organism can continue for long to exist sanely under conditions of absolute reality. Even larks and katydids are supposed, by some, to dream. Hill House, not sane, stood by itself against the hills, holding darkness within; it had stood so for eighty years and might stand for eighty more' to King's 'It's probably wrong to believe there can be any

limit to the horror which the human mind can experience. On the contrary, it seems that some exponential effect begins to obtain as deeper and deeper darkness falls […] And the most terrifying question of all may be just how much horror the human mind can stand and still maintain a wakeful, staring, unrelenting sanity'.

2. This is true of the source novel too, when the moment that Louis's sanity finally fully slips – a moment that we have clearly been headed towards since Gage's death – is accompanied by a '(!CLICK!)' that is 'the sound of some relay fusing and burning out forever, the sound of lightening stroking down in a direct hit, the sound of a door opening' (1983: 453).

3. An interesting addition to this set of films is *Anything for Jackson* (Justin G. Dyck, 2020), which features grieving grandparents who wish to resurrect their dead grandson through a pregnant stranger.

4. This trauma also, arguably, influences the appearance of Zelda in Rachel's visions. It is highly unlikely that Zelda – who had spinal meningitis – looked in life the way she appears to Rachel, and I would argue that Rachel's visions are shaded through the memory of her traumatised eight-year-old self, who saw Zelda as monstrous.

Chapter 2: 'Couldn't plant anything here but corpses anyway': contextualising *Pet Sematary*

In his study of cinematic adaptations of Stephen King's work, Simon Brown explains that accounts of these films 'tend to be almost exclusively decontextualized in favor of a text-based comparison of the preoccupations of specific films', essentially 'removing them from the wider contextual discussions around the horror genre and the industry' (2018: 6). Following Brown, it is my intention here to situate Stephen King and adaptations of his work as intrinsically part of the fabric of 1980s horror, with a consideration of shifts both subtle and seismic that were occurring around the genre and the industry at this time.

In the 1980s, horror had become more popular than ever, with a growth in production meaning that the genre was a 'consistent juggernaut in box office competition' (Muir, 2007: 6). In addition to this, horror had gained a new visibility through three key developments: the emergence of specialist fan magazines; an increasing acknowledgement of the work of special effects makeup artists (which was legitimised in both fan publications and by the Academy); and the VHS explosion. This chapter will begin by outlining how these developments all contributed to this new visibility of horror, how this then led to a greater level of critique being directed at the genre (and the effect this critique had on popular perceptions of it) before moving on to explore the genre as it stood in the 1980s more broadly. In doing so, this chapter will pull away from a focus on slasher cinema and video nasties to illuminate the varied directions the horror genre expanded in during the decade, and will examine where the Stephen King "brand" fits within this genre context. Finally, this chapter will close by analysing the ways in which *Pet Sematary* specifically both adheres to, and departs from, the tropes and conventions of 1980s horror cinema and, in doing this, will firmly recontextualise *Pet Sematary* as a key entry in both Stephen King adaptations and 1980s horror.

'THERE'S SO MUCH BLOOD!': *FANGORIA*, SPECIAL EFFECTS AND VHS

Fangoria magazine was first published in 1979, the year between genre classics *Halloween* (John Carpenter, 1978) and *Friday the 13th* (Sean S. Cunningham, 1980). It was originally conceived of by Kerry O'Quinn and Norman Jacobs as a fantasy film-based publication to complement their existing science fiction orientated *Starlog*.[1] The welcome note from Kerry O'Quinn in the magazine's first issue underlines this intended focus, proclaiming that 'our intention is for *Fangoria* to be the first classy, professional, pictorial news magazine covering the world of fantasy' (O'Quinn, 1979: 4). This emphasis on the fantasy genre is easily discerned in the pages that follow, with features on *Dr Who* (BBC, 1963–), *Battlestar Galactica* (ABC, 1978–1979), fantasy animation, and fantasy art. Alongside this, however, sits a short interview feature with special effects artist Tom Savini regarding his work on *Dawn of the Dead* (George A. Romero, 1978), complete with an accompanying image of an exploding zombie head special effect from the film. A short feature on *The Amityville Horror* (Stuart Rosenberg, 1979) is also included, along with an article on *The Creature from the Black Lagoon* (Jack Arnold, 1954), and a retrospective on the career of Christopher Lee. This split focus between fantasy and horror in the first issue of *Fangoria* is perhaps what led a reader to write to the magazine in time for the second issue's letters page, citing Kerry O'Quinn's welcome note statement that the magazine would centre on fantasy, but concerned that it had articles 'only on horror films' (Malmquist, 1979: 6). Although there was a subtle shift in the magazine's focus within its early issues from primarily fantasy to primarily horror, it would not be until the seventh issue of *Fangoria* that coverage of the fantasy genre would be dropped almost entirely. Issue 7 of *Fangoria*, with a cover image of Jack Nicholson in his role as Jack Torrance in *The Shining*, introduced more gore to the publication, and featured an extended article on *Maniac* (William Lustig, 1980), with several full colour (and quite graphic) photos of the special effects work of Tom Savini from the film.

Fangoria had seemingly come to a crossroads, and this movement towards an alignment with the more shocking (and wonderfully icky sticky) aspects of horror cinema led to two reader's letters in issue 9, which questioned the necessity of gory photographs in the magazine. One reader stated

> Okay, you went way overboard in issue #7. I mean the *Friday the 13th* scenes in #6 were okay, but those *Maniac!* [sic] Scenes were totally repulsive! What makes you think that any normal person wants to see that scalping effect! [...] Keep showing such totally sick scenes and I'll stop buying *Fangoria*. I'm sure many people will agree.
>
> (Hicks, 1980: 5)

The other reader, a John Landis of California (never heard of him), similarly notes that, although he generally enjoys the content of the magazine, that 'Gore, for its own sake, quickly grows tiresome. Please try to refrain from repeatedly printing the most gruesome stills you get your hands on' (Landis, 1980: 5).[2] *Fangoria*, however, only amped up the gore from issue 7 onwards, with cover features on *Scanners* (David Cronenberg, 1981) for issue 10, *Friday the 13th: Part II* (Steve Miner, 1981) for issue 12, and *An American Werewolf in London* (John Landis, 1981) for issue 14, all accompanied by detailed pictorial articles. The letters from readers questioning the graphic imagery in the magazine slowly became scarce,[3] particularly after issue 11, wherein several readers wrote in to defend and champion the graphic photos present in the magazine.

The broader cultural impact of *Fangoria*, then, is in part due to this willingness to transgress what could be considered "good taste" in the magazine marketplace. This resulted in a reputation that stretched internationally, with the UK Prime Minister Margaret Thatcher holding up a copy of the magazine in Parliament and condemning it as 'absolutely appalling', before proposing banning *Fangoria* under the Obscene Publications Act of 1959 (Lanzagorta, 2006). Horror has, historically, been a genre often met with disdain or, in Harry M. Benshoff's words, is one that is 'somewhat ghettoized in popular culture as a critic-proof, low class, low-budget exploitation genre aimed at thrill seeking teenagers' (Benshoff, 2014: xiii). Horror fans, by extension, have been traditionally characterised as deviant, moronic, 'sick or stupid (or sick and stupid)' (Hutchings, 2004: 83).[4] *Fangoria*, by aligning itself with what one reader's letter calls the 'cheap, sensational, blood-letting, gore-gushing' (McLaughlin, 1981: 5) aspects of the genre, actively situated itself in opposition to what could be considered more "mainstream" tastes. And, in their consumption of the magazine, early avid *Fangoria* readers and readers since, have – consciously or not – set themselves in opposition too. To paraphrase music critic Lester Bangs, *Fangoria* fans used the magazine to form their own good tastes.[5]

Despite a lack of scholarly work on the publication (a critical neglect that has recently started to be addressed through work such as Webster (2022)) and its impact on the horror genre,[6] it is clear that *Fangoria*'s influence is strong and long-lasting. While several publications followed in its wake in the late 1980s, such as *Gore Zone* and *Toxic Horror* – both sister publications to *Fangoria* from the creators of *Starlog* – as well as *Deep Red*, *Slaughter House*, and *Horror Fan*, it is important to remember that, for most of the decade, *Fangoria* was one of the only sources of in-depth information on contemporary horror production available to fans. This unique element of the magazine was underlined in former editor Michael Gingold's proclamation that in the 1980s 'we were the only guys visiting the set of a horror movie' (quoted in Collis, 2017).[7] *Fangoria*'s 'eclectic and equal coverage of both large and small releases' (Williams, 2013: 112) no doubt played a part in the taste formations of many American horror fans of the time. But, on the negative flipside of this, *Fangoria*'s unique position meant that it held a great influence over how films were reported on and subsequently received by audiences. This may have had some effect on the canonisation of certain horror films above others. Perhaps most significantly, however, *Fangoria* spearheaded what Ernest Mathijs has called a 'paradigmatic shift' in 1980s horror cinema in terms of the status of special effects (Mathijs, 2009: 153).

Although special effects have always been key to the horror genre, the early 1980s saw the release of two films that are still widely held as the gold standard in terms of pioneering practical horror effects: *An American Werewolf in London* and *The Thing* (John Carpenter, 1982). The special effects for *An American Werewolf in London* were the first to be honoured by the Academy Awards for Best Makeup and Hairstyling, a category created perhaps in response to complaints that the Academy had failed to acknowledge the groundbreaking prosthetic effects present in *The Elephant Man* (David Lynch) in 1980 (Valenti, 2020). And, although not well received by audiences of its time, with it being called (among other things) 'instant junk' (Canby, 1982: 14), and criticised for 'sacrificing everything at the altar of gore' (Ansen, 1982: 73), *The Thing* continues to be a cultural touchpoint for practical effects in the horror genre several decades after its release (see Figure 6).[8] Both Rick Baker and Rob Bottin, the respective special effects makeup artists for these films,[9] featured regularly in *Fangoria* and were part of the publication's focus on the work of special effects makeup artists more generally. This coverage included effects artists both famed and lesser known. Lance Anderson's work on *Parasite* (Charles Band, 1982), for example, is featured in issue 19 – with Anderson going on, with his son David Anderson, to create the special effects for *Pet Sematary*. As Daniel Martin has observed, *Fangoria* was crucial in terms of the increasing attention being paid to developments in special effects within the horror genre and the magazine was particularly central to the rise of body horror. Martin notes, for instance, that *Fangoria* was 'devoted to an appreciation of this new explicit horror that was being met with derision and disgust by the mainstream press, and mainstream audiences' (2015: 48). Gore, now more graphic than ever due to evolving special effects, had arguably become 'the central organizing principle of horror films in the 1980s' (Kendrick, 2014: 310), and it was gore's transgressive presence in the genre that *Fangoria* revolved around in this decade. For the casual reader, it may have seemed that all 1980s horror had to offer was blood and carnage.

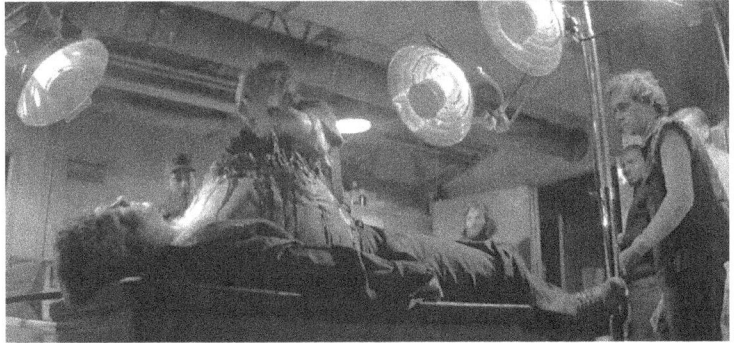

Figure 6. 'Instant junk'/horror classic The Thing

Fangoria's position, as 'the magazine that "had the guts to show you the guts"' (Williams, 2013: 111) was bolstered by the detailed full colour photographs within its pages, lending 'a frisson of the forbidden to the magazine, which contributed much to its immediate popularity' (Williams, 2013: 113). *Fangoria*, and to an extent other publications such as *Cinefantastique*, played no small part in the repositioning of special effects artists as the rock stars of the horror genre, with former *Fangoria* editor Bob Martin noting in issue 10 of the magazine that a future issue may contain a feature on 'the makeup man as the new auteur of horror' (Martin, 1981: 4). Along with its focus on special effects, it would be fair to say that Stephen King was also a central presence in the pages of *Fangoria* during the 1980s too. Detailed coverage of each King adaptation, along with mentions of – and interviews with – the author were contained in a great number of issues from the time, and I will be exploring the magazine's engagement with *Pet Sematary* in Chapter Four. All of these elements position *Fangoria* as a key contributor to the growing visibility of the horror genre more broadly within the decade, right on the shelves of your local newsagent.

Another key development in this visibility of the horror genre is the popularity of VHS as a new media format. VHS's rise to prominence was relatively fast and, as Stephen Prince notes, 'Yearly sales of VCRs jumped from 802,000 in 1980 to 11–12 million per year during the second half of the decade' (2002: 94). Despite this boom in sales of VCRs, the price point of VHS tapes was high, which led to the widespread emergence of video rental businesses. In response to the demand for VHS, horror distribution companies filled video store shelves with not only high-profile releases but cheaply made shot-on-video horror too. The saturation of the VHS market demanded attention-grabbing box art to ensnare passing customers, and the horror sections of video stores became galleries of sorts, with films such as *Driller Killer* (Abel Ferrara, 1979), *Cannibal Holocaust* (Ruggero Deodato, 1980), *Anthropophagus* (Joe D'Amato, 1980), and *The Evil Dead* (Sam Raimi, 1981) among others bearing striking covers that seemed to promise that the content of the film would be equally as macabre or extreme.[10] As Linda Badley argues, there was a growing sense in some quarters that horror had "invaded" rental stores, and was now 'virulent and uncontrollable', with VHS being the catalyst that had 'activated and spread whatever plague the genre was born from', while 'encouraging its impulse to return to the wound site, [and] replay the "nasty bits"' (2009: 46).

This distinctive and noticeable presence of the genre in video stores led to several moral panics. In America, influential film critics Roger Ebert and Gene Siskel dedicated an entire episode of their popular programme *Sneak Previews* (PBS, 1977–1996) to what they termed the 'Women in Danger' subgenre, otherwise known as the slasher film. After naming several films such as *I Spit on Your Grave* (Meir Zarchi, 1978), *When A Stranger Calls* (Fred Walton, 1979), *The Silent Scream* (Denny Harris, 1980), *Don't Answer The Phone!* (Robert Hammer, 1980), *He Knows You're Alone* (Armand Mastroianni, 1980),

Motel Hell (Kevin Connor, 1980), *Phobia* (John Huston, 1980), *Mother's Day* (Charles Kaufman, 1980), and *Schizoid* (David Paulsen, 1980), Siskel asserts that a commonality of these films is their focus on women 'being raped [and] being sliced apart'.[11] Later in the programme, Ebert denounces the women in danger strand as 'violent, extreme, grotesque, nauseating […] right off the map of any kind of good taste', before suggesting that to enjoy these films was to be a 'vicarious sex criminal'. Meanwhile, in the United Kingdom, the new visibility of the horror genre resulted in the video nasties panic of the early 1980s. Highlighting the horror genre as a place of explicit violence, tabloid headlines in the United Kingdom told how 'High Street Horror is Invading the Home' (Chippindale, 1982), in what was termed a wholesale 'Rape of Our Children's Minds' (Hebdige, 1983). Articles such as these would usually go on to describe the lurid – and often incorrect – content of various "nasties". This media furore, fuelled by the self-appointed moral guardian Mary Whitehouse and her pressure group the National Viewers' and Listeners' Association, resulted in the banning of seventy-two films. The video nasties panic and the slasher subgenre have been covered extensively in horror scholarship, but less discussed, perhaps, is how varied the landscape of horror produced in the 1980s really was.

'We had an awful good time': 1980s horror cinema

Despite the media tempest around the potentially damaging effects of horror cinema, and the clear positioning of the genre as a place of transgressive content by the tabloid press of the time, retrospective scholarly accounts of the genre in the 1980s have often, in contrast, framed the decade's horror as 'deeply conservative – some would say reactionary' (Towlson, 2014: 163), and as 'an era pathologically affirming conservative family values' (Williams, 2015: 193). John Kenneth Muir, for instance, goes as far as to note that, although they were lambasted by moral guardians, slasher films of the decade in particular appeared to be 'designed and executed as conservative precautionary tales', which – in their punishment for pre-marital sex, drinking, and drug taking – 'actually toed the party-line with dedication' (2007: 11). Other accounts have observed that, in comparison to 1970s horror, which was 'steadily more progressive, [and] constantly challenging the legitimacy of capitalist, patriarchal rule', 1980s horror cinema abandoned this sensibility to become reflective of "neoconservative" culture (Sharrett, 1993: 100).

We begin to see a wider picture emerging here, in which the horror genre of the 1980s is framed as lurid and potentially dangerous by tabloid newspapers and eminent film critics of the time and then, conversely, as crushingly conservative by more contemporary film scholars. No matter the position, accounts from both camps appear to argue that horror cinema of the 1980s was an indistinguishable mass, considering it to be 'a decade that lacked originality and good taste' (Fahy, 2019: 104) and one that had little room for variance or innovation. Although several accounts have sought to recuperate this period of horror history (see for example Trecansky, 2001; Gill, 2002; Kvaran, 2016), there is still a distinct tendency towards a homogenisation of the decade's horror output as 'a glut of slashers, [and] a surfeit of "rubber reality" (the successor to the slasher paradigm)', where the 'quality is not so high as it appeared in the 1970s' (Muir, 2007: 15). Whereas the 1970s is often framed as something of a 'golden age' for horror cinema, critics and scholars alike have asserted that, in contrast, there is 'little to salvage' from the genre in the 1980s (Wood, 2003: 169). The prevalent opinion seems to be that the horror genre had 'abandoned the gritty, countercultural sensibility of the previous decade' (Fahy, 2019: 104) for campy, interchangeable slasher films, with scholars who had previously championed the ability of the genre to act as a vehicle for social commentary in the 1970s conversely dismissing 1980s horror output. One such example is the film theorist Robin Wood, who queried whether, aside from *Day of the Dead* (George A. Romero, 1985), there was '*any* American horror movie made since 1980 that could be championed as any sort of radical statement about our impossible (so-called) civilisation?' (2004: xviii, emphasis in original). Whereas Wood had written extensively on the political power of 1970s American horror cinema, he made his position regarding its 1980s counterpart clear in his suggestion that, instead of discussing the 'development' of the genre it was more fitting – post 1980 – to examine horror's 'degeneration' (2004: xiii). Moreover, a great number of accounts argue that the decade's horror films were 'vapid, sensationalised, and redundant' (Fahy, 2019: 104), with the genre being oversaturated with 'seemingly endless' sequels (Grant, 1992 [2015]: 229) and 'reductive exploitation films'; both strands being dependent on 'spectacular special effects and gory bloodbaths of promiscuous (mostly female) teenagers' (Williams, 2015: 192). This narrow view of the genre not only discounts the technological and industrial upheavals I have detailed thus far, but also ignores the varied content, themes, and subgenres present within the horror genre during this time.

Box office horror hits such as *The Exorcist* (William Freidkin, 1973) and *Jaws* (Steven Spielberg, 1975) in the early 1970s, and the recent success of both *Halloween* in 1978 and *Friday the 13th* in 1980, encouraged major studios to engage with the genre in the 1980s. In fact, despite James Kendrick's assertion that member studios of the Motion Picture Association of America avoided the production and distribution of horror cinema in the decade, leaning instead 'towards productions that had some air of respectability' (2014: 311), several major studios – including Paramount, Universal, Warner Brothers, and Columbia Pictures – were quick to branch into the slasher subgenre. Paramount in particular, the production company responsible for *Pet Sematary*, maintained a steady output of horror films throughout the 1980s, including seven *Friday the 13th* sequels.

Although the slasher subgenre was an incredibly popular format in the early part of the 1980s, and its presence at the forefront of moral panics may explain its prominence in scholarly work on the decade, to focus on this subgenre alone is to discount several other strands of horror cinema that developed and stretched in wildly different directions during the decade. This included more family friendly horror such as *Poltergeist* (Tobe Hooper, 1982), *Ghostbusters* (Ivan Reitman, 1984), and *Gremlins* (Joe Dante, 1984), along with teen-horror such as *The Monster Squad* and *The Lost Boys* (Joel Schumacher, 1987). More adult orientated but still "horror-lite" entries such as *Fright Night* (Tom Holland, 1985) could also be placed in this category. On a seemingly diametrically opposite strand, splatter horror such as *Basket Case* (Frank Henenlotter, 1982), *Evil Dead II* (Sam Raimi, 1987), and *Street Trash* (J. Michael Muro, 1987) took advantage of the developments in special effects makeup and prosthesis detailed earlier in this chapter, as did body horror entries like *The Fly* (David Cronenberg, 1986) and *Society* (Brian Yuzna, 1989), which showcased the talents of special effects artists such as Chris Walas and Screaming Mad George respectively. Conversely, ghosts and hauntings are at the centre of *The Changeling* and *The Entity* (Sidney J. Furie, 1982), with these films among others largely eschewing gore effects. Vampire and werewolf films such as *An American Werewolf in London*, *The Howling* (Joe Dante, 1981), *Near Dark* (Kathryn Bigelow, 1987), and *The Hunger* (Tony Scott, 1983) both honoured and reinvigorated classic horror monsters. Creature feature films such as *Ghoulies* (Luca Bercovici, 1985) and *Critters* (Stephen Herek, 1986) joined genre entries such as *Night of the Creeps* (Fred Dekker, 1986) in mixing horror with comedy, while other hybrid films such as *The Terminator* (James Cameron, 1984) and *Predator* (John McTiernan, 1987) blended horror, sci-fi and action genre conventions. Of course, this is but a small sample of the variety of horror films produced in the 1980s, as space does not permit a full filmography and evaluation of the decade's genre output, and there are various entries I have not included here, particularly in terms of independent horror productions and smaller cycles such as the possessed doll movie (see *Dolls* (Stuart Gordon, 1987), *Child's Play* (Tom Holland, 1988), and *Puppet Master* (David Schmoeller, 1989)). Notably, and most relevantly for this book, however, is the recurrence throughout the 1980s of films based on works by Stephen King.

'A MAN GROWS WHAT HE CAN, AND TENDS IT': THE KING OF THE DECADE

In the 1980s, there was what has been termed as a 'spate' of Stephen King adaptations (Waller, 1987: 10), with fourteen films based on his work being released between 1980 and 1989.[12] Some of these, such as *Christine* (John Carpenter, 1983), followed closely on the heels of their source novel's publication,[13] and three films based on Stephen King stories were released in 1983 – the year of *Pet Sematary*'s publication – alone. John Kenneth Muir has argued that the horror genre in the 1980s can be characterised as an era in which 'name brand movies' became both popular, and also crucial marketing tools (2007: 13), proposing that 'One visit to a local video store in the 1980s, and a fan could easily and safely gravitate to a *Friday the 13th* sequel or a *Halloween* sequel and be assured of a certain level of quality. Name recognition trumped an untried, untested quantity every time' (2007: 14). Muir goes on to single out Stephen King as the ultimate 1980s brand name, noting the success of *Carrie* (Brian De Palma, 1976) and positing that Hollywood continually attempted to recreate this film's success, with the idea being that 'If King's books were bestsellers, why couldn't films based on his books be blockbusters' (2007: 14). Although obviously not a franchise as such, it is true that there were a large number of King adaptations released in a short space of time but, as Simon Brown rightly notes, despite "Stephen King" as a literary brand being well established by the 1980s, his name as a cinematic brand took slightly longer to coalesce (2018: 61). In order to properly understand the cultural currency of what Brown has termed 'Brand

Stephen King' (2018: 61) within the 1980s, however, it is first necessary to return briefly to the previous decade.

Figure 7. From top left, the trailers for Carrie, The Dead Zone, Maximum Overdrive, *and* Silver Bullet

King's first published novel, *Carrie*, was released in 1974, and was swiftly followed by Brian De Palma's cinematic adaptation of the story in 1976. De Palma's adaptation was not only a box-office success, but received widespread critical acclaim, with its stars Sissy Spacek and Piper Laurie being nominated for Academy Awards. Early cinematic adaptations such as *Carrie* and *The Shining* did not foreground King's name in their marketing. In a survey of original trailers (see Figure 7), it is telling that in the trailer for *Carrie* Stephen King's first name is misspelled as 'Steven' and only appears briefly in the final moments of the advertisement. And, in the trailer for *The Shining*, his name only appears under Stanley Kubrick's directorial credit, positioning Kubrick as the true "auteur" of the work instead.[14] It is not until the release of *Creepshow* (George A. Romero, 1982) that King's name is placed prominently in a trailer, with a voiceover noting that the film was created by 'the author of *Carrie*, *The Shining*, and *Cujo*'. As the cinematic adaptation of *Cujo* (Lewis Teague, 1983) had not yet been released at this point we can assume this trailer is not referring to the films based on these books, but the books themselves. This possibly demonstrates that there was still a need to rely on King's literary – and highly profitable – brand a while longer.

It is around this time though that we see a movement towards the establishment of a cinematic brand Stephen King, with tertiary materials around *Creepshow* underlining his involvement, and the positioning of King, along with George A. Romero, as one of the leading names in the horror genre at this time. This can be seen, for example, in a 1982 cover for *Cinefantastique*, where King and Romero, along with prominent special effects artist Tom Savini, are accompanied by the caption 'Are these the scariest men in America?'

By 1983, the trailers for *Cujo* and *The Dead Zone* (David Cronenberg, 1983) displayed King's name clearly, with *Cujo* featuring it in blood red block capital letters. Within the trailer *for The Dead Zone* – although the film was directed by David Cronenberg who was, at this point, well known in the horror genre – we see the first King adaptation to use the prefix 'Stephen King's', clearly framing King as the creative force behind the work. This demonstrates King's growing cultural capital in cinematic terms as a brand. Although this prefix was then not present in the trailer for *Christine*, it returns for *Children of the Corn* (Fritz Kiersch, 1984), *Firestarter, Cat's Eye* (Lewis Teague, 1985), and *Silver Bullet* (Dan Attias, 1985).

In 1986, *Maximum Overdrive*, King's first – and to date only – foray into directing an adaptation of his own work was released. It is here that we see what could be considered the first peak of the cinematic brand name of Stephen King. The trailer for *Maximum Overdrive* is introduced by King himself, who stands in near darkness with his back to the "Happy Toyz" vehicle from the film, a black Western 4800 truck replete with a Green Goblin head on the grille. King addresses the audience directly, noting that 'a lot of people have directed Stephen King novels and stories, and I finally decided if you want something done right, you ought to do it yourself'. As King speaks, clips from the film are shown, and the Green Goblin's eyes begin to ominously glow red. King continues, stating that 'I just wanted someone to do Stephen King right', and assuring he is going to 'scare the hell out of you, and that's a promise'. These allusions to doing Stephen King 'right', may well be related to King's well-documented distaste for *The Shining*, which I will explore further in Chapter Four.

Despite King's promises, however, *Maximum Overdrive* was met with critical disdain, being described as 'nonsense' (Variety Staff, 1985), 'dreary to the max' (Goldstein,

1986), and a 'mess' (Kogan, 1986: 3). Even King himself would later describe the film as a 'moron movie' (quoted in Magistrale, 2003: 20). The critical failure of *Maximum Overdrive* in 1986 stood in stark contrast to the acclaim won by – and financial success of – *Stand By Me* in the same year, an adaptation that could – by virtue of its position as a drama perhaps – be distanced from Stephen King's name and horror "brand" in its marketing. As much as it is the site of the peak for the first wave of Stephen King adaptations, then, 1986 can also be seen as the tipping point at which "Stephen King" lost its impact in Hollywood, a trend that continued until *Pet Sematary*. As critic Glenn Lovell remarked in 1988, 'King's stock in Hollywood is down. His name no longer assures box office success' (quoted in Herron, 1988: 224). More damningly, Michael Collings ventured a year earlier that 'associating King's name with a film almost automatically endangers the project' (1987: 63). This new distaste Hollywood had for King was apparently mutual and, as one of the screenwriters of *Stand By Me*, Raynold Gideon, commented, by the mid-1980s, 'King was kind of dead in Hollywood and at the same time he had soured on Hollywood' (quoted in Matthews, 2005: 70). Although production of films based on stories by Stephen King did not shudder to a halt, with *Creepshow 2* (Michael Gornick) and *The Running Man* (Paul Michael Glaser) both being released in 1987, the former film saw a sharp fall in box-office takings compared to *Creepshow*,[15] and the latter – which could be distanced from King's brand due to its minimal horror elements – only did moderately well. It would seem that by 1988 the era of Stephen King's cinematic brand had stalled. What then, did *Pet Sematary* – which made no effort to distance itself from King's name and brand and, if anything, embraced that connection[16] – have to offer that overcame the commercial and critical failures related to the Stephen King cinematic brand of the mid-1980s?

'I'M SURE THINGS WILL BE FINE': *PET SEMATARY*'S SAMENESS, DIFFERENCE, AND NIHILISM

When asked about his and fellow writer/director John Campopiano's decision to focus on *Pet Sematary* in their documentary *Unearthed and Untold: The Path to Pet Sematary* (2017), Justin White remarks that the film has a quality that 'separates it from other popular horror films of the era' (quoted in Coffel, 2018). This positioning by White, of *Pet Sematary* as distinct from other 1980s horror, can also be seen in the insistence of producer Richard P. Rubenstein at the time of the film's release that *Pet Sematary* 'stands apart from the more standard horror fare being offered' (Szebin, 1989a: 6), and in Mary Lambert's resolve that '*Pet Sematary* is not a slasher movie' (Szebin 1989b: 122), through which she distances the film from the decade's most lucrative subgenre. Although I would agree that *Pet Sematary* is perceptibly different from the previous horror films of the decade, I propose that this is through its nihilism rather than any explicit rejection of dominant 1980s horror conventions, with the film striking a careful balance between what was possibly expected from a horror film of the time while drawing its overarching tone from the previous decade's genre output.

Zombies had remained a perennial presence in the genre during the 1980s, with the third zombie film from George A. Romero, *Day of the Dead*, appearing in 1985, and films such as *Dead and Buried* (Gary Sherman, 1981), *Night of the Comet* (Thom Eberhardt, 1984), *Return of the Living Dead* (Dan O'Bannon, 1985), *Return of the Living Dead Part II* (Ken Wiederhorn, 1987), and *The Video Dead* (Robert Scott, 1987) among a host of others proving the living dead's cultural currency throughout the decade. Although it could be argued that Timmy Baterman, Rachel, and Gage are not quite the same as the zombies that bite and rend their way through *Day of the Dead*, they are still revenants from beyond the grave, and their abject quality is clear. In fact, in the source novel Jud wonders aloud how to classify Timmy Baterman, and states, 'Maybe it was a zombie' (1983: 306). Similarly, just before Louis digs Gage's body up in the cemetery, he contemplates how Gage will return and asks himself 'Do you want to resurrect a zombie from a grade-B horror picture?' (1983: 323). Skilfully created by David and Lance Anderson, the "zombies" of *Pet Sematary* leak bodily fluids, are violent towards the living, and display graphic bodily injuries, such as Timmy's decayed appearance (see Figure 8) and Rachel's mutilated face, exemplifying what Phillip Brophy terms a 'graphic sense of physicality' that was characteristic of horror in the 1980s (1986 [2000]: 280). Additionally, although not a zombie, Pascow too haunts the film with his brain – wet and sticky looking – clearly visible through his crushed skull. While it is true that the gore in *Pet Sematary* is not as explicit as that found in *Reanimator* (Stuart Gordon, 1985) for instance, and much is often made of the restraint exercised by David and Lance Anderson in relation to this (particularly in terms of the appearance of the Gage-creature at the end of the film), the appearance of zombie-like creatures in *Pet Sematary* and the violence visited upon characters by them would not be out of place in a multitude of horror films from the era.

Figure 8. Timmy Baterman's zombie like appearance

The inclusion of songs from The Ramones – alongside Elliot Goldenthal's sweeping orchestral and choral score – add a distinctly 1980s punk rock feel to *Pet Sematary*. The incorporation of a punk band's music within the film adheres to a trend towards using alternative, metal, or rock music in the horror cinema of the decade, placing *Pet Sematary* in the company of *Friday the 13th Part VI: Jason Lives* (Tom McLoughlin, 1986), which featured music from Alice Cooper, *Trick or Treat* (Charles Martin Smith, 1986), the soundtrack of which was recorded by Fastway, Dokken's inclusion in *A Nightmare on Elm Street 3: Dream Warriors* (Chuck Russell, 1987), and *Return of the Living Dead*, the music from which is made up of songs from multiple punk bands including The Cramps, 45 Grave, and The Damned. The basic narrative conventions of *Pet Sematary* are also not particularly unique when viewed against other horror cinema entries of the decade. The inclusion of a cursed Native American burial ground – discussed at length in Chapter Three – had already been seen in *The Amityville Horror* and *The Shining*, and while the death of a child was perhaps unusual in the 1980s it was not unheard of and had been shown in *Halloween III: Season of the Witch* (Tommy Lee Wallace, 1983) and the remake of *The Blob* (Chuck Russell, 1988) among other films. Other elements, such as the jump scares utilised by the film and the presence of a prophetic ghost (as can be found, for example, in *An American Werewolf in London*) are also not unique to *Pet Sematary*.

Despite Jeffery Weinstock's assertion that the film is 'comforting in its conclusions' (2008: 41), I argue that the distinct quality that *Pet Sematary* possesses, and the aspect that sets it apart from other horror entries of the 1980s, is in fact its unrelenting nihilism. It is also this thematic preoccupation that distances the film from other King adaptations of the decade, where usually, 'Although good individuals do not always survive [...] good always triumphs over evil, be it natural, supernatural, or part of a diseased American society' (Brown, 2018: 43). While the Creed family, when they arrive in Ludlow, seem happy and without any obvious familial tensions – unlike the already troubled families of *Carrie* or *Cujo* – the film unremittingly depicts the sadness after sadness, and horror after horror, they endure. This tonal quality of *Pet Sematary* brings it more in line with examples of horror cinema from the previous decade, and films such as *The Last House on the Left* (Wes Craven, 1972) and *The Texas Chain Saw Massacre* (Tobe Hooper, 1974), which used 'overt nihilism – in a period of extreme cultural crisis and disintegration' (Wood, 1979: 76). Although a division can be drawn, with *Pet Sematary* not having as much of an overtly political slant as films such as *Dawn of the Dead* or *The Hills Have Eyes* (Wes Craven, 1977), Pamela Craig and Martin Fradley have previously argued that the striking quality of late 1960s and 1970s horror 'is less their articulation of any kind of coherent politically oppositional stance and more their (entirely symptomatic) outright nihilism' (2010: 97). This is something that *Pet Sematary* possesses in abundance. Unlike the end of *The Shining*, *Cujo*,[17] or *Silver Bullet*, there is no uplifting coda or monster vanquished at the film's close, which ends with the deaths of all but one of the Creed family, who will surely be traumatised for life. This nihilistic tone of the narrative was recognised by King himself, who suggested that 'It seems to be saying nothing works and nothing is worth it, and I don't really believe that' (quoted in Murphy, 2017). This nihilism contributed to the sense that *Pet Sematary* was a different beast to the Stephen King adaptations that had come before it, even as it maintained a connection to a variety of the overarching conventions of 1980s horror more broadly.

This chapter has sought to firmly contextualise *Pet Sematary* in the horror genre as it stood in the 1980s; a genre that gained an increased level of visibility due to several developments both inside and outside of the film industry. This new visibility, however, was at the cost of a concurrent increase in the attention paid to the genre and criticism of it. The longstanding effects of this have included the continuing (and reductive) categorisation of horror as a genre that is both exploitative and moronic. It is perhaps little wonder then that the creators of *Pet Sematary* sought to distance themselves from the horror genre, and also from previous King adaptations. The success of King adaptations had peaked and fallen in a matter of a few years, and they were increasingly seen as a site of diminishing returns. At the same time, the film perhaps adhered to broader genre conventions, such as zombies and a punk rock soundtrack, as horror was still clearly full of box-office promise. Regardless of the reasons behind *Pet Sematary*'s simultaneous sameness to and difference from horror cinema of the 1980s, this was at least partially responsible for its success, and this success was, in turn, key to the reinvigoration of the cinematic brand of Stephen King.

Notes

1. *Fangoria* was originally going to be called *Fantastica* but following a court case with the creators of *Fantastic Films* – another fantasy-based publication – regarding the similarity of their titles, the magazine was duly renamed *Fangoria*.
2. Given that he does not exactly avoid bloody scenes in his own productions, and the fact that the letter was entitled 'A Solicited Letter', Landis's comments should be taken with a pinch of salt.
3. A particularly amusing letter from issue 10 however reads 'There is, or used to be, a distinction between horror films and atrocity films, a distinction that Gene Siskel seems to understand a whole lot better than you do. If the distinction is ever re-established, and the domains of nightmare are reclaimed from the goremongers, it will be thanks to people like him, *no thanks at all to your sort*' (Peoples, 1981: 5, emphasis added).
4. This historic denigration of the genre has, of course, led to several instances where films that are – for all intents and purposes – part of horror cinema have been distanced from the genre by tastemakers and critics, followed by subsequent criticisms of these attempts by scholars (see for example Jancovich, 2001; Edwards-Behi, 2017, McMurdo et al, 2019).
5. This is paraphrased from Bangs's statement regarding paracinema, in which he states 'Nobody likes movies like *Teenagers from Outer Space* or *Wrestling Women vs. The Aztec Mummy* save any loon sane enough to realise that the whole concept of Good Taste is concocted to keep

people from having a good time, from revelling in a crassness that passeth all understanding [...] But fuck those people who'd rather be watching *The Best Years of Our Lives* or *David and Lisa*. We got our own good tastes' (1988: 122–123). I should note here, however, that it is not my intention to debate if the horror genre is a form of paracinema.

6. Although, in the 1980s, Phillip Brophy astutely drew a connection between the magazine and developments in the contemporary horror film (1986 [2000]: 277).

7. It is of course worth noting that although *Fangoria* is perhaps the most famous, it was not the first horror-specific publication, with an important predecessor found in *Famous Monsters of Filmland* magazine.

8. Steven Kostanski, co-director of *The Void* (Steven Kostanski and Jeremy Gillespie, 2016) for example, noted in an interview that he hoped the practical effects in the film were a 'throwback' to *The Thing* and *The Fly* (Dickinson, 2015).

9. Interestingly, Rob Bottin started his career as Rick Baker's assistant, and took over from Baker on special effects duty on *The Howling* on Baker's recommendation when he left the production to work on *An American Werewolf in London*.

10. The books *Shock! Horror! Astounding Artwork from the Video Nasty Era* (Brewster, Fenton, and Morris, 2005) and *The Art of the Nasty* (Wingrove and Morris, 2009) both stand as fantastic records of this time in box art, and as excellent nostalgia trips.

11. It is worth noting that the majority of these films do not contain scenes of rape.

12. I have included *Creepshow*, *Cats Eye*, and *Creepshow 2* in this number, as although they contain original segments that were written by King for their respective films, they also contain segments based on existing King work.

13. *Christine* was released a mere eight months after the publication of the novel.

14. It is interesting to note that the 1997 miniseries adaptation, which was directed by Mick Garris, was billed as *Stephen King's The Shining*, perhaps as an attempt at reclaiming the story. For an in-depth examination of the tensions between King and Kubrick regarding *The Shining*, see Mee (2017).

15. Worldwide, *Creepshow* made $21,028,755 against *Creepshow 2*'s $14,000,000. A comparison of their domestic opening weekends shows *Creepshow* making $2,286,812 more than its sequel film.

16. The trailer to *Pet Sematary* includes intertitles that forefront King's involvement, naming him "The King of Horror", "The King of Terror", "The King that scares you the most", before a voiceover notes the film is 'Stephen King's all time best-selling tale of horror'. The trailer underlines this connection with the 'Stephen King's...' prefix.

17. I am referring here to the film *Cujo*, not the novel, which has a markedly more tragic ending.

Chapter 3: 'The ground is sour': analysing *Pet Sematary*

Although Stephen King began writing *Pet Sematary* in 1979 (Winter, 1989: 152–156), the finished novel was not unleashed onto the public until November 1983. This delay, for a writer as prolific as King, is unusual, as is the fact that after completion the book languished in a drawer in King's office for an extended period of time. King commented to Douglas A. Winter shortly before the book's publication that he felt he had 'written something that was so horrible that [he] didn't want to deal with it on a redraft' (quoted in Winter, 1982: 106). King later noted that the book was only published as a way for him to break his contract with Doubleday, the publishing house responsible for his earlier works, and to remove himself from their author investment plan (Breznican, 2019a). King has been very vocal about his animosity towards the story since its release, noting in 1985 that 'If I had my way about it […] I still would not have published *Pet Sematary*. I don't like it. It's a terrible book – not in terms of the writing, but it just spirals down into darkness' (quoted in Murphy, 2017). Despite King's misgivings about the novel, and his reluctance to publish it, it went on to become a bestseller, outstripping the performance of his previous novels at the time. Just as there was an extended period of time between the writing of *Pet Sematary* and its publication, several circumstances and delays – which will be examined in more depth in Chapter Four – led to a five-year gap between the publication of the *Pet Sematary* novel and the filmic adaptation being released in April 1989.[1]

As stated in Chapter One, many previous accounts focusing on *Pet Sematary* make much of its similarities to older Gothic tales such as *Frankenstein*, but any reader hoping to find those comparisons here will be left disappointed. Although grief is the theme that has absolute centrality in *Pet Sematary*, to present this as the sole concern of the story would be to do a disservice to both *Pet Sematary* the novel and *Pet Sematary* the film. This chapter therefore will begin by highlighting the presence of boundaries, both literal and metaphorical, within the narrative, before moving on to analyse two themes – the family and the "Indian Burial Ground" – that are both key to *Pet Sematary*, and resonant to the ten-year period that elapsed between Stephen King starting work on the novel, and Mary Lambert's cinematic version of the story.

'THE BARRIER WAS NOT MEANT TO BE CROSSED': THE BOUNDARIES OF *PET SEMATARY*

Pet Sematary is a film predicated on boundaries. The Creed's house, for example, backs onto an untamed wilderness and within these woods are both the harmless pet cemetery and its ancient doppelganger, the Micmac burial ground. These two sites are separated by a mass of fallen trees and branches, with this deadfall marking the line between what is known to Louis – his house, his family, Ludlow – and an unknowable territory. The deadfall also acts as the most significant visual boundary line within the film, and is referred to as a 'barrier' by the ghost of Victor Pascow on his first visitation to Louis. The road that lays between the Creed house and the home of their neighbour, Jud, is another visual boundary and one that features as the site of several key moments in the film: the Creed family first meet Jud at the roadside, after he saves Gage from toddling into the path of a truck as they move in to their new home; Church's death on the road is the main inciting incident in the story; and, of course, Gage's demise on that road later in the film acts as the turning point of the narrative. The road is also a boundary that Louis Creed traverses several times during the film, each time in a markedly different mental state. The Louis that crosses the road that first night – to share a beer with his new friend, Jud – is a far cry from the Louis that crosses over to kill his reanimated son, or indeed the Louis that makes his way back over the road afterwards with the body of his mutilated wife, determined that he can bring her back and that 'it'll work this time'. Less tangible boundaries exist within *Pet Sematary* too, such as the line between life and death, and the barrier between sanity and madness that Louis hurtles towards and crashes over during the course of the film.

The line between wakefulness and dreaming becomes less and less defined as the narrative unfolds. The first sequence that we might assume to be a dream occurs after the death of Victor Pascow. That night, Louis wakes to find Pascow in his and Rachel's bedroom, and follows him downstairs and then to the pet cemetery. Once Pascow has given Louis his terrible warning about the deadfall – the barrier 'not meant to be crossed' – Louis falls to his knees on the ground, pleading that 'I just want to wake up, that's all', and startles awake in his own bed, momentarily comforted that it was all just a bad dream. He throws back the bedcovers only to discover that his feet and legs are caked in mud, suggesting that his encounter with the dead teenager was actually real.

Louis is not the only Creed to be caught dreaming, however, and, along with Ellie having a precognitive encounter with Pascow in a nightmare, Rachel experiences powerful dream-like visions of her dead sister, Zelda. As Louis successfully manages to dig up Gage's body and cradles the dead child to his chest, we cut to a scene showing a hallway in Rachel's childhood home, where she is staying with Ellie. The camera is at a canted angle and shows the myriad of photographs on the walls – the significance of which I will return to momentarily – in disarray. Rachel enters the back bedroom, where Zelda – who had spinal meningitis – lived during her illness and died within, only to find Zelda laying on the bed. Zelda has been shown in previous flashbacks to have very limited ability to move, due to her painfully twisted spine, but despite this she suddenly snaps bolt upright into a sitting position – accompanied by a gruesome bone-snapping noise – and faces Rachel. The camera pushes in slowly as Zelda tells Rachel 'I'm coming for you Rachel, and this time I'll get you. Gage and I will get you, for letting us die'. Rachel, terrified, leaves the room as Zelda cackles maniacally. This too, however, is suggested to be a dream, followed as it is by Rachel waking suddenly on the plane back to Maine. This dream/reality line is troubled more thoroughly later in the film however when Zelda appears for a second time to Rachel when she is fully awake (albeit sleep deprived and in a state of extreme emotional distress) in Jud's bedroom. Zelda scuttles across the floor before promising Rachel that she is going to twist her back 'so you'll never get out of bed again', and it is this encounter with her dead sister that leaves Rachel open to Gage's subsequent attack. This scene is imbued with dream logic, not only in the presence of the long-deceased Zelda, but also through the presentation of Gage, who wears a dark velvet tunic and trousers, carries a walking cane, and wears a top hat. The first time we see a version of this outfit in the film it is worn by Zelda during one of Rachel's flashbacks, and we also see it on a child in a painting hung at Rachel's parent's house (see Figure 9).

Mary Lambert has spoken of her love of dream logic and her desire to incorporate it into her films (with *Siesta* (1987) being a prime example of this), and has noted that she decided not to include an explanation for this recurrent outfit in *Pet Sematary* within the narrative, stating that 'I don't believe you need to say those things out loud [...] they just need to be there visually' (Breznican, 2019b). She has also commented that her intention was to hint at the idea that the malevolence residing in the burial ground is 'working through all these machinations' in its quest to destroy the Creed family (Breznican, 2019b), and that her inspiration came from *memento mori* photography. Lambert has noted that these photographs, which were taken of dead loved ones to have as family keepsakes, were 'a form of bringing someone back from the dead' (Breznican, 2019b), and had the painting we see in Rachel's childhood home created specifically for the film by Marlene Stewart, the costume designer for *Pet Sematary* (Tangcay, 2020).

Photographs play an important role in *Pet Sematary* and along with the use of still images during Gage's death scene – where a montage of photographs of Gage from his birth to his most recent birthday flash in front of the audience in lieu of the aftermath of the accident – they are also a prominent presence in the scene directly after, strewn across the table where Louis sits. There is an interesting difference here between this scene and the aftermath of Gage's death in the source novel, where – after we have read about Gage's death, his funeral, and Jud's story of Timmy Baterman – King provides us with a whole chapter detailing an alternative version of events. In this chapter, Louis manages to catch Gage before he gets to the road, and we vicariously experience the boy's movement from school to Johns Hopkins University. We are told he became a tall, sweet, adult who met a girl and converted to Catholicism before making the

Figure 9. The recurring outfit throughout Pet Sematary

Olympic swimming team and winning the gold medal for the United States. The chapter ends with Louis waking from this dream and his returning horror at the fact that his son is dead. Whereas the novel textually presents the "what might have been", *Pet Sematary* the film presents us visually – through the use of photographs – with the "what was", which is now forever lost. Additionally, following Gage's death, Ellie insists on carrying a picture of her brother around with her, and Rachel's parent's house is also full of photographs showing generations of the Goldman clan, almost to an uncomfortable degree (see Figure 10). Portraits fill the hallways of Rachel's childhood home, giving the sense that she is 'engulfed in photographic memories' when she visits her parents (Luers, 2016). Photography features in more discreet ways throughout the film too, such as Rachel observing a photograph of Jud as a younger man just before she is killed, and when Louis contemplates an image of a healthy, smiling Pascow clipped to his student file after his death. The same scene shows a prominent framed picture of Gage and Church – who will both die before the film concludes – on Louis's desk. The photographs in *Pet Sematary*, therefore, shift slowly from reminders of happy times in the life of the Creeds to reminders of time passing, and of the inevitability of death. Photographs, and their uncanny ability to bridge the gap between present and pastness, and life and death, return at key moments of the *Pet Sematary* story, which is haunted by the omnipresence of a returning past.

Figure 10. Rachel's childhood home is filled with photographic memories

'EACH BURIES HIS OWN': THE FAMILY AND FATHERHOOD IN *PET SEMATARY*

The period between *Pet Sematary*'s inception as a novel and its release as a feature film encompasses an era of brewing social unrest in the United States. It included the final years of Jimmy Carter's term in presidential office, the subsequent presidency of Ronald Reagan, and the first few months of George H. W. Bush as America's president. It is also characterised by a figurative return to conservativism and the rise of the New Right. With the (now terribly familiar) campaign slogan 'Let's Make America Great Again', Reagan's Republican Party placed a massive ideological emphasis on the importance of the family unit (Schulman, 2001; Leppert, 2019), positioning the nuclear family as 'the building block of society' (Rossinow, 2015: 2). Following his first term in office, which ran from 1981 to 1984, Reagan's second campaign for election played into the idea that 'the economy soared, the Soviet Union faltered, and American patriotism surged' (Troy, 2005: 15). The accompanying advertisements underlined how families could 'look forward to the future' in a country that was now 'prouder, and stronger, and better' than before. There was a growing emphasis during Reagan's presidency on an idealised return to the 1950s and traditional family values and structures, with that past decade being seen as 'the high point of American family life' (Marcus, 2004: 40). This cultural turn towards the 1950s at the end of the 1970s and into the 1980s can be seen too in pop culture products of the time such as *Happy Days* (ABC, 1974–1984) and *Back to the Future* (Robert Zemeckis, 1985). It was argued that the feminist and gay liberation movements of the 1960s and 1970s had contributed to a breakdown in the structure of the American family, with traditional gender roles reassigned or shifting, and divorce rates rising. This led to the proposal of the Family Protection Act in 1980, which was intended to 'stop federal attacks on traditional values, and included tax breaks for those families in which wives did not work outside the home' (Marcus, 2004: 56). The Act promised to invalidate laws pertaining to domestic abuse, and reintroduce restrictions around teaching about homosexuality in public schools, as well as dismantling gender equity efforts.

Within both Ronald Reagan and his successor George H. W. Bush's campaigns, there was a recurrent invocation of the concept of the American Dream, to which the family is key. Reagan's 'Prouder, Stronger, Better' campaign commercial for the 1984 elections in particular has been described as possessing 'a haze of nostalgia and optimism', containing images that could easily slot into a 1950s sitcom (Beschloss, 2016). This return to 1950s idealism extended into the presidency of Bush, who had served as Reagan's vice-president.[2] Bush emerged in 1989 – the year of *Pet Sematary*'s release – as a president who was also a strong celebrater of what Allen Hunter has termed 'suburban pastoralism', and the belief that the 'suburban, middle-class family [...] was the natural unit of society, upon which the rest of the social order rested, and for which it was organised' (1987: 104). This focus on the family and pastoralism as intrinsic to the American Dream was foregrounded in several of Bush's 1988 campaign commercials, in which he is surrounded by young children at family barbeques and while walking through green fields, and presented as a benevolent father figure for the nation.

Figure 11. Clear blue skies and promises of friendship

The first time we meet the Creed family in *Pet Sematary* they seem to represent the American Dream realised. They pull up in a station wagon to a large, well-kept house, and a bumper sticker alerts us to the fact that the driver is an MD – a well-paying white-collar job. The house is deemed 'gorgeous' by Rachel, a stay-at-home wife, as their first-born child, Ellie, plays on a tyre swing in the front garden. Although the idyllic scene is punctured by their youngest child, Gage, wandering too close to the road, he is safely corralled and scooped up by Jud, the Creed's new neighbour. Even as Jud responds to Rachel's queries about the path to the side of the property and the music becomes slightly more ominous, the sky behind the characters is blue and clear (see

Figure 11), and the scene ends with a friendly clap on the shoulder and the promise of intergenerational friendship for Louis Creed and Jud.

Mary Lambert has made much of the Maine geography featured in the film, and how it emphasises the pastoral ideal, with this being situated in *Pet Sematary* as a picturesque counterpoint for the dark forces that lay in wait beyond the deadfall. The locations in *Pet Sematary* include Ellsworth (where both Jud's and the Creed family's houses were located), Mount Hope Cemetery in Bangor (where Missy's funeral was held and Louis robs Gage's grave), and parts of both Bucksport and North Hampden can be seen as the Orinco truck drives on its way to end Gage Creed's life. Along with a location in Sedgewick being used as the setting of the Micmac burial ground, various areas in Seal Harbor and Mount Desert Island in Acadia National Park are travelled through by Louis and Jud on the way there. Lambert has stated that 'I dragged the crew all over Maine looking for these locations', (Lambert, 2019) and remarked on the fairy-tale quality of the Maine landscape: a characteristic she was keen to highlight in the film. Lambert explains that Maine had an 'iconographic quality, this archetypal resonance', and that similarly, she wanted the Creeds to be presented as 'the archetypal family', with Gage in particular needing to be 'perfect' (Lambert, 2019). It is significant that the point at which the family are captured at their most Elysian, in a scene almost Rockwellian in its evocation of the American Dream, is also the point at which their lives are ripped apart by Gage's brutal death, and the dark force within *Pet Sematary* starts to creep into the rips and tears left behind (Figure 12).

Figure 12. Pastoral scenes in Ludlow, Maine

Gage's death scene begins with a sweeping shot that establishes the enormous amount of ground that surrounds the Creed home. Behind their sizable yard, we can see water sparkling in Youngs Bay, the woodland beyond that, and, in the foreground, a bright red kite is flown by Louis. In the background, Rachel, Ellie, and Gage sit at a gingham-covered picnic table with Jud. After encouraging Gage to join him in flying the kite, Louis turns to laugh at an outburst from Ellie and does not notice Gage dropping the kite spool and running to catch up with it. A crane shot shows both Gage's pursuit of the spool and the Orinco truck that is almost level with the house. Finally alerted to Gage's position by Rachel and Jud, Louis takes off in a sprint but falls just shy of reaching his son (Figure 13). A succession of quick edits show: Gage in the forefront of the frame with the truck fast approaching; the shocked reaction of the driver as he sees Gage in the road; the driver's feet hopelessly stamping on the brakes; Gage's face as the camera zooms in, imitating the fast-forward motion of the truck; and then the underside of the truck as it ploughs into him. A shot follows of the kite being tugged down from the sky, accompanied by the sound of the locked brakes screeching.

Figure 13. Louis fails to catch Gage

A slow-motion sequence, of Gage's tiny bloodied sneaker bouncing along the asphalt and Louis's agonised scream, closes the scene. The horror of Gage's death punctuates the most pastoral moment in the whole film, and, as Lambert explains, it serves to emphatically underline the fear of what could happen, in 'that one moment where you turn away from your beautiful perfect son, to look back at your beautiful perfect wife, on a beautiful perfect day' (Campopiano and White, 2017). The Creeds enter the film as Reagan's American Dream made flesh; a loving couple consisting of a housewife and a doctor, with two children – a boy and a girl – and a family cat. They live in a gorgeous house opposite a kindly older neighbour with whom they strike up an instant friendship, and take part in activities like picnics in their sprawling back garden, which has a picturesque view. The Creeds even have a white picket fence (which, had it gone all the way around the front yard, would have proved incredibly useful). But, despite the fact that both Reagan and Bush emphasised the safe, stabilising properties of the family unit, and even though Louis moved his family from the urban Chicago to the pastoral Ludlow to protect them 'from modernity's uncertain hand' (Dymond, 2013: 789), death finds them here too, and it is perhaps this very move that led to the deaths of Gage, Rachel, and Louis.

Several critics have argued that the destruction of the Creed family in *Pet Sematary* is due to a dereliction of parental duty, and that Gage's return as a murderous revenant is an example of 'innocent monsters created by irresponsible adults' (Alegre, 2001: 105). Particular blame seems to be laid squarely at the feet of Louis and his failure as a father (see Schroeder, 1987; McAleer, 2011; Dymond, 2013 to name only a few). There are four fathers, or father figures, that feature in *Pet Sematary*, namely Louis, Jud, Irwin Goldman (Michael Lombard), and Bill Baterman. In the film, Louis mentions his own father once, at the funeral of Missy Dandridge, and in the source novel it is explicitly stated that he died when Louis was three – a similar age to Gage.[3] Louis Creed, therefore, has so far navigated fatherhood with little in the way of a template, and his desire to prove himself in this familial role, not just for his own benefit but to prove Rachel's father, Irwin, wrong, is central to his character. The friction that exists between Louis and Irwin Goldman is shown in several scenes. For instance, Louis's distance from his in-laws is clear when he refuses to join his family in travelling to Chicago for Thanksgiving, and, after Rachel argues that it is 'supposed to be a family holiday', answers that 'as far as your dad is concerned, I'm never going to be a member of this family'.[4] As much as the Goldmans seem hostile towards Louis, this antipathy is reciprocated, as is made clear when Rachel recounts her traumatic experiences with her seriously ill sister Zelda and Louis muses that 'If I ever needed another reason to not like your father and mother I have one now'. The hostility between the Goldman and Creed fathers reaches fever pitch at Gage's funeral, when Irwin confronts Louis over the child's death. Irwin's fury grows as he shouts that

> I knew something like this would happen. I told her when you were first married, you'll have all the grief you can stand and more, I said. And I look at this, I hope you rot in hell. Where were you when he was playing in the road? You stinking shit! You killer of children! You son of a bitch!

A scuffle ensues and, in the melee, Irwin crashes into Gage's coffin, knocking it from its bier and sending it to the ground. For a brief second, the lid snaps open, allowing Louis – and the audience – a glimpse of Gage's hand before the lid closes again. The specific sorrow of a father that has lost his son, represented too in the story of Bill and Timmy Baterman, is painfully etched into Louis Creed, and previous scholars have asked if Louis's response would be the same if Ellie had died instead (Dymond, 2013: 805).[5] Vivian Sobchack, meanwhile, has argued that as much as infants represent the future, they also represent the past, in that within them, 'familiar identity and family resemblance are produced as visible traces of the past's presence in the present and ensure the past's presence in a future safely contained and constrained by tradition and history', noting furthermore that a child will 'at best [...] carry the father's name forward – at least, his seed' (1987 [2015]: 176). Gage's death, therefore, means that Louis not only loses his son but also part of himself, and any assurance of a form of immortality through Gage outliving him.

Given that the 1980s was a decade that 'witnessed a redefinition of fatherhood' (Carroll, 1990: 185), it is unsurprising that a large number of horror films from the time sought to grapple with this 'crisis of masculinity within the American family' (MacKenthun, 1998: 98–99). Various fathers in North American horror cinema at this time were presented as, at best, inept or at worst, outright evil. Examples of this include possessed fathers such as George Lutz of *The Amityville Horror*; those risen from the grave for revenge like Nathan Grantham in *Creepshow*; murderous stepfathers such as Jerry Blake in *The Stepfather* (Joseph Ruben, 1987), or perfectly nice but totally ineffectual dads like Steve Freeling of *Poltergeist*, Donald Thompson of *A Nightmare on Elm Street* (Wes Craven,

1984), or Rand Peltzer in *Gremlins*. The recurrent prominence of fathers within the wider horror genre in the 1980s – particularly in contrast to the lack of parental figures featured in slasher films of the time – can be seen, as Vivian Sobchack suggests, as one of the ways that the horror genre sought to 'overtly interrogate paternal commitment and its relation to patriarchal power' (1987 [2015]: 180). What is certain is that Stephen King returns to fathers and fatherhood often in his work, with the most famous King-created father possibly being Jack Torrance in *The Shining*, an aspiring writer whose sanity disintegrates under the influence of the Overlook Hotel and who then attempts to murder his wife and child. Although Louis seeks to restore his family, rather than destroy it, his very efforts to do so serve as the downfall of the Creeds. Louis is not a bad man or even a bad father – at least certainly not in the tradition of fathers in other Stephen King stories. He is not a violent alcoholic in the vein of Jack Torrance, not abusive like Alvin Marsh of *It* (1986), or a sexual predator like Tom Burlingame in *Gerald's Game* (1992). Instead, Louis's hamartia is his single-minded belief that he is doing the right thing and what is best for his family, even when all evidence points to the contrary.

Although Jud is often read and understood as a father figure to Louis in *Pet Sematary*, and it is arguably his intention to take on that role, it is precisely his interventions into the lives of the Creed family that lead to more heartache. Mary Lambert has previously argued that she sees Jud and Victor Pascow as opposing 'angels' within the narrative, with Pascow – despite his horrific appearance – being the 'good angel' in his desire to help the Creeds, and Jud – a seemingly kindly older neighbour – as the 'bad angel' that opens Louis's mind to dreadful possibilities (Lambert, 2019). Jud's secretive and possibly manipulative/manipulated nature is revealed in the scene directly following the burial of Church in the Micmac ground, where he tells Louis not to share details of what has happened with Rachel, and notes:

> What we did, Louis, was a secret thing. Women are supposed to be the ones who are good at keeping secrets. But any woman who knows anything at all will tell you, she's never seen into a man's heart. The soil of a man's heart, Louis, is stonier – like the soil up there in the old Micmac burial ground.

Although Louis's actions – keeping Jud's explanation of the burial ground and the resurrection of Church secret – are unacceptable, his intentions are seemingly (almost) pure or at the very least understandable. Louis has failed in his fatherly duty to protect Ellie from upset or harm and Jud's intervention gives Louis the opportunity to delay the inevitable death of Church and assuage his guilt. His resurrection of Gage too, stems from his culpability in the child's death due to his inattention and his failure once more to protect his family. Even his final resurrective act with Rachel reads as a last-ditch – and insane – attempt to retain some semblance of a nuclear family through any means possible (Figure 14).

Figure 14. Louis's fragile hold on sanity is slipping fast

Although many have asserted that the film's narrative 'indicates that the Creed's misfortunes are entirely man-made', with Rachel's trauma and both her and Louis's carelessness being the real evil of the narrative (Kord, 2016: 65), what is missing from this perspective – and indeed what T. S. Kord touches upon but does not fully unpack in her analysis – is the role of the Micmac burial ground. As much as Louis may be blinded by the power that the ground has, and makes increasingly terrible decisions based on this, we see throughout the film that the ground, and perhaps even the landscape of Maine itself, has an omniscient influential power over the Creeds, lending a fatalistic edge to the narrative. As mentioned in Chapter One, the death of Gage has an awful inevitability to it, seemingly set in motion from the moment he toddles near the road in the first scene of the film, and various moments in the narrative point towards a predestined path having been chosen for the Creeds. Jud watching for Louis and then falling asleep at the precise moment Louis carries Gage's body to the burial ground and missing his window of opportunity to intervene,[6] or the tyre on Rachel's car blowing as she races home, sending her careening into a tree, are both examples of this influence.[7] This is underlined further when Rachel leaves the car, and Pascow materialises behind her to warn that 'It's trying to stop you, do you hear me? It's trying to stop you!' Although it is never directly stated in the film what 'It' is, there is no doubt where 'It' lives: deep within the Micmac burial ground.

'THAT'S THE WAY THE INDIANS DID IT': BEYOND THE DEADFALL LIES A PROBLEMATIC TROPE

Part of the appeal of Stephen King's work has been said to be his ability to create a thoroughly recognisable America. Rebecca Janicker argues, for instance, that King's 'intricate blending of real-life locations with a detailed fictional geography […] supplies a degree of authenticity' to his narratives, and is key to his popularity (Janicker, 2007: np). This sense of familiarity is underlined by King's use of common American brand names. *Pet Sematary* the novel, for example, is full of references to McDonalds and Hefty bags, while in the film logos such as those for Pampers and Budweiser are prominently on display. There is clear effort in both versions of the story to serve the audience a slice of recognisable Americana. The "American-ness" of *Pet Sematary*, however, runs deep, and its engagement with American history is seen most clearly in the positioning of the Micmac burial ground as a key – or perhaps *the* key – location in the story.

Before I begin, I wish to make it clear that in my discussion of the Micmac burial ground and its inclusion in *Pet Sematary*, I do not seek to – nor could I – speak on behalf of the indigenous people of North America. As I will detail below, Native American burial grounds have featured in horror stories since the mid-1800s at least, leading Joe Nazare to propose that 'the Native American might be seen as just another variable to be plugged into horror's xenophobic formula: establishing a monstrous Other which must be vanquished to preserve cultural order' (2000: 24). Nazare's reduction of the whole of the horror genre to xenophobic aside, I will argue that the obviously problematic trope of "The Indian Burial Ground" within *Pet Sematary* is one that is informed and influenced by what was occurring in the social-political climate surrounding the creation of both the novel and the film. The presence of the ground in the narrative – which was interestingly erased for the most part in the 2019 remake[8] – also hopefully provides space to engage with America's colonial and genocidal past, subjects that are being increasingly broached in broader horror cinema and that are central to the New England location of *Pet Sematary*.

Darryl V. Caterine has traced the myth of "cursed Indian land" back to nineteenth-century Puritan writings, the majority of which stemmed from New England due to the great immigration of Puritans to that area between 1629 and 1640. He suggests that this idea of 'damnable terrain' can then be tracked to the horror tales of H. P. Lovecraft – which often detailed New England landscapes haunted by ancient evil – as well as the work of others such as Robert E. Holland.[9] Caterine both deduces that the idea of cursed land became 'a distinctive myth of American cultural origins' and that 'feeling terrorized by the ground beneath one's feet became, for some, a hallmark of being an authentic American' (2014: 38). Horror cinema has featured cursed lands countless times, but in terms of specifically Native American land being cursed there are several prominent and well-known examples.[10] *The Amityville Horror*, for instance, is based on Jay Anson's 1977 book of the same name. The book – based on the alleged paranormal experiences of the Lutz family during their residence at 112 Ocean Avenue – claims that the house was built on a site used by the Shinnecock people as an enclosure for their sick and dying; despite a lack of evidence for this claim, and the fact that the Shinnecock lived fifty miles away (Dickey, 2016). The filmic adaptation of the book also contains this erroneous mythology. Following just a year later, Kubrick's *The Shining* contains a line describing how the Overlook Hotel is 'supposed to be located on an Indian Burial Ground'. The presence of the burial ground is not brought up again, and is not stated in the film to have any connection to the events that transpire, although it is perfectly possible to pick up on this implication.

With an origin dating back to a treaty between the Passamaquoddy community and the State of Massachusetts in 1794 (Barnum, 2010: 1165), Maine had been the site of a series of legal battles regarding the ownership of 60% of the land within the state since 1972 (Dickey, 2016). These became the basis of the Maine Indian Claims Settlement Act of 1980, wherein the Passamaquoddy, Penobscot, and Maliseet communities were federally recognised and presented with a settlement of $81.5 million to enable them to reacquire

300,000 acres that had been historically stolen from them (Paterson, 2012: 195). This was the first successful suit 'for the return of any significant amount of land' (Kempers, 1989: 290), and inspired a series of future legal suits. Other legal confrontations that were ongoing throughout the 1980s aimed for the federal recognition of several other tribes, such as the Mi'kmaq.[11] Tom Tureen, who acted as a lawyer for the Passamaquoddy, Penobscot, and Maliseet communities, described this point in history as 'a nasty and disillusioning time in Maine' (quoted in Brodeur, 1985: 108). This is a sentiment supported by Andrew Akins, the chairman of the Passamaquoddy-Penobscot Negotiating Committee, who recalled that the land claims caused a gamut of emotion in the state. White people's reactions in particular, felt as though:

> We had touched a raw nerve that extended back into the innermost recesses of the true personality of the white people around here and unleashed all their deep hatred for Indians, together with guilt for what they had done to the Indians over the years. We had been invisible for so long, you see, that the whites simply couldn't conceive that we had any rights except those they chose to confer on us. Well, we're not invisible any longer.
>
> (quoted in Brodeur, 1985: 134)

I wish to stay a moment with Akin's quote, and particularly his use of the term 'invisible'. Within *Pet Sematary*, and indeed within *The Amityville Horror* and *The Shining*, there are no Native American characters, despite the presence of "Indian Burial Ground" (Figure 15). This is perhaps most striking in *Pet Sematary*, where the burial ground plays such a key role. Moreover, the absence of Native American people is never explained within the narrative aside from a line that 'they stopped using that burial ground when the ground went sour'. Scholars such as Gesa Mackenthun (1998), Joe Nazare (2000), and Michelle Raheja (2011) have argued that Native American people are often rendered an absent presence in horror fiction despite a noticeable preoccupation within the genre on their culture, mythology, and customs. This 'violence of invisibility' (Raheja, 2011: xii) not only serves to occlude Native American voices from the genre, but also shapes wider cultural perceptions. The burial ground in *Pet Sematary*, for example, is presented as an unknowable – and inherently evil – place and as such, even in their absence, Native Americans are figured as an antagonistic force. In other films, such as *Wendigo* (Larry Fessenden, 2001), Western interpretations of complex indigenous mythological figures tend to reduce them to Others whose narrative purpose is to be defeated by overarchingly white casts.[12]

Figure 15. The burial ground

Renee L. Bergland has suggested that the specter of Native American forced dispossession 'haunts the American nation and the American imagination. But, in spite of the national guilt and horror that Indian ghosts signify and inspire, American writing invokes them obsessively' (2000: 5). The recurrence of Native ghosts and legends may also, as Bergland goes on to state, assist in the construction of what it means to be 'American' (2000: 19). Gesa MacKenthun also centralises national guilt in her reading of this fascination and proposes that the 'Indian exodus [...] produced a greater psychological instability within U. S. society than is generally assumed' (1998: 97). A great deal of this instability revolves around the concept of ownership or territory and, according to Carol Clover, the city/country axis that pervades a great deal of horror cinema is essentially a version of the "Indians"/Settlers conflict of 1940s westerns, with both narrative conflicts acting as opportunities to acknowledge national guilt (1992 [2015]: 134). Bergland reads this differently, however, and argues for the 'surprising power' of the theme of dispossession within horror cinema, stating that while 'Europeans take possession of Native American lands, to be sure [...] at the same time, Native Americans take supernatural possession of their dispossessors' (2000: 3). It is Louis's tampering with the Micmac ground (which is not knowable to him, as a non-Native person) that brings destruction upon his and his family's heads. The reclamation of Jud's home by the land it is built on in the film's final act – with moss, mould, and fungus covering surfaces and furniture sinking into the ground – and the association between Native Americans and the very soil of Ludlow is perhaps one of the clearest allegories in the film (see Figure 16). This reclamation, along with Jud's accompanying voiceover that 'what you buy is what you own, and what you own always comes home to you' illustrates the themes of ownership and possession (both physical and spiritual) that permeate *Pet Sematary*. It is true too that although there are ghosts in the film – Pascow and Zelda – the presence of the ancient burial ground haunts the Creeds far more thoroughly than they ever could. As Colin Dickey purports, the presence of the burial ground engages with a specific anxiety around land ownership in America and the fact that 'Embedded deep in the idea of home ownership – the Holy Grail of American middle-class life – is the idea that we don't, in fact, own the land we've just bought' (2016).[13] These themes are also especially relevant when positioned against the cultural context of Maine at the time of the novel's, and the film's, creation.

Figure 16. Jud's house is reclaimed by the land

Tensions around land ownership and the mistreatment of Native American burial sites and culture in North America are still ongoing. In 1990, for example, land disputes that had dated back to the 1800s in Oka, Canada, came to a climax when a golf club announced plans to expand their course, which already bordered on land used by Mohawk people for burials. In another incident in 1995, the building of a mill in Port Angeles, Washington uncovered ancestral Native remains, with a portion of these being 'removed to be later used as fill' (Boyd, 2009: 713). More recently still, the remains of over 750 Native people – mostly children – were uncovered in unmarked graves in the province of Saskatchewan in Canada, on the site of a church-run boarding school that existed for the purpose of assimilating Native youth (BBC, 2021).[14]

Pet Sematary's use of a Native American burial ground is no doubt both an extractive process and highly problematic. Although the presence of this trope can function to comment on ideas around ownership and territory in North America, the traumatic history of the country has since found new expression in horror cinema created by Native American people themselves, with films such as *Blood Quantum* (Jeff Barnaby, 2020). Although it could be argued that the three themes I have presented here as central to *Pet Sematary* – boundaries, the family, and the "Indian Burial Ground" – represent King's authorial preoccupations, and are indeed common to horror cinema more generally, the latter two resonate clearly with the period of time in which *Pet Sematary* was written and then adapted to film. It is no surprise, in an era seemingly obsessed with the family, that *Pet Sematary* – as a horror film – systematically dismantles this institution. The concept of the American Dream too, is seen in *Pet Sematary* to be built on a graveyard of national trauma.

Notes

1. This too is unusual. *Carrie*, for example was published in 1974 and followed by De Palma's adaptation a mere two years after. *The Shining*, too, had a rapid turnaround from novel to film, with King's book being published in 1977 and Kubrick's film arriving in 1980. Perhaps the quickest however, as mentioned in the previous chapter, was *Christine*, with a mere eight months between novel publication and filmic adaptation.

2. George H. W. Bush also served as the vice-president between 1981 and 1989, during Reagan's time as president.

3. King himself was around this age when his father left (Adams, 2000).

4. The relationship between Louis and his father-in-law is expanded in the book. For example, where Louis recounts an evening where Irwin offered to pay Louis a large sum of money on the understanding that he would then no longer see Rachel.

5. This is a question partially answered in the 2019 adaptation. Louis's grief process is slightly different in this newer film and his descent into madness seemingly much quicker. However,

the character of Ellie is more of a central character in *Pet Sematary* 2019. She is also slightly older, and her relationship with Louis is underlined by several scenes where he spends time with her. His relationship with Gage in *Pet Sematary* 2019 is consequently deemphasised as a result. It is also worth noting that Ellie's death in the 2019 film – where she is lured into the road by Church – is quite different from Gage's in the 1989 film, where Louis's inattention plays a much larger role.

6. This is something that is missing for the most part from the 2019 remake – Jud falling asleep at the exact time that results in him missing Louis travelling to the Micmac ground with Gage for example (which happened in both the novel and the 1989 film) is altered in the 2019 adaptation to Louis drugging Jud's drink to ensure he cannot intervene in Gage's resurrection.

7. Pascow too seems to possess some kind of influence over his surroundings, such as when he holds the door at the airport to allow Rachel to board a connecting flight during her desperate attempt to get home. This is complicated, however, by the fact that, near the end of the film, Louis walks straight through him on his way to the Micmac Ground. Whatever influence Pascow possesses, however, pales into insignificance in comparison to the hold the Micmac Ground has on Ludlow.

8. In the 2019 remake, there is no introduction of the ground as 'Micmac' from Jud when he and Louis arrive at the site to bury Church, but there is a short conversation between the two men later in the film regarding 'local tribes' and their belief in the Wendigo. There is also a scene where Louis consults a map on the internet that shows a portion of the area near his house ominously labelled as 'Tribal Land'.

9. Specifically, his short story *The Horror from the Mound* (1932).

10. *Poltergeist* is often mistakenly thought to contain an "Indian burial ground". It is in fact emphatically stated by property developer Mr Teague that the land he is building on is 'not ancient tribal burial ground, it's just people'. Although why he thinks this will make anyone feel any better about it is unclear.

11. The Mi'kmaq people are indigenous to the north-eastern area of Maine and are also present in areas of Canada. It is therefore interesting that King chose the name 'Micmac' for his fictional (and absent) Native American community in *Pet Sematary*, which is set in a more southern area of Maine.

12. The Wendigo does feature in the novel *Pet Sematary* and in the original script – it is absent from the 1989 adaptation; however, a small discussion of the Wendigo is featured in the 2019 version and it is strongly hinted to be present when Louis buries Ellie in the sour ground.

13. Interestingly, this theme of ownership and boundary lines is covered slightly more in the 2019 adaptation. Over dinner, Rachel asks Jud if she and Louis 'own' the pet cemetery. Jud

replies that 'it's part of the property', which is a line taken almost verbatim from the novel. Within the novel this is expanded still, as this exchange concludes with Louis inwardly pondering that 'own' and 'part of the property' are not quite the same thing.

14. These are, unfortunately, only a scant few examples in the recent history of interference with and desecration of Native land in North America.

Chapter 4: 'A place where the dead speak': authorship and the production of *Pet Sematary*

CEO of Blumhouse Productions, Jason Blum, stated in October 2018 that he was yet to produce a horror film directed by a woman because 'There are not a lot of female directors period, and even less who are inclined to do horror' (Patches, 2018). Although Blum was quick to apologise and does indeed seem to be actively addressing the lack of diversity in terms of directors for Blumhouse-produced films, his statement underlines what seems to be a universally acknowledged (and inaccurate) truth – women and horror do not mix.

Several scholars have noted that women directors are often assumed to have been hired in order to offset genre expectations. Laura Mee, for example, explains that in the case of Mary Harron's adaptation of *American Psycho* (2000), 'the involvement of female filmmakers was […] promoted as a corrective measure' (2020: 92) due to the misogynistic violence found in the source novel. Kimberly Peirce, the director of *Carrie* (2013) – who joins Mary Lambert in the very small "women who have directed a Stephen King adaptation club"[1] – was also thought to have been hired to bring a 'female perspective' to the project (Paskiewicz, 2017: 3). There is an assumption that a woman director brings a distinct 'softness' to a production, a belief that Julia Ducournau, the director of *Raw* (2016), was stunned at, stating 'Have you seen my movie? Did you see it? How can you say it? I'm not toilet paper. Toilet paper is soft. I am not soft' (quoted in Godfrey, 2017). The discourses around women who direct horror tend to focus on the 'exceptional – and often "morbid" nature of both their tastes and their practice' (Paskiewicz, 2017: 43), particularly if their films have a sizeable budget or reach some degree of success. Ducournau, for example, after winning the Palme D'or award for her sophomore feature *Titane* (2021) at the Cannes Film Festival, was asked how she felt about being thought of as a 'provocateur' whose work is 'purposefully shocking for the sake of being shocking', to which she responded 'I think if I were a man, nobody would say that. How many men direct horror movies that are so much more graphically shocking than what I do? I mean, seriously, I'm sick of it' (Handler, 2021). It would seem then that a woman's name being attached to a horror project not only invites speculation on her credentials for directing such a film, but intense focus on the film itself, and attention being paid to whether or not a certain 'femininity' is imbued in work directed by women. Rachel Talalay, for instance, when directing *Freddy's Dead: The Final Nightmare* (1991), received notes from the studio urging her to make her film 'less girly' (Century, 2018). This desire to discern a 'femaleness' to filmic products created by women results in disappointment when seeming expectations of what a film helmed by a "woman director of horror" should be are not met, as can be seen in Tosha Taylor's insightful comment that Talalay is 'not the mythological ideal of the feminist horror director simultaneously sought after and condemned by critics' (2020: 78).

Mary Lambert's position, as the first woman to helm a Stephen King adaptation, and for a major studio no less, certainly gave rise to speculation. After outlining historical perspectives of the relationship between women and horror, this chapter will detail the genre context from which Lambert emerged as one that was largely perceived as a masculine space – perhaps more so than any other decade – despite the clear presence of women creators in the genre at that time. Regardless of her gender, Mary Lambert is presented here as an important figure, not only in terms of her contributions to the horror genre, but as the person who put the Stephen King brand back in cultural favour as the genre headed into the 1990s.

'THE GROUND YOU BURIED HIM IN': WOMEN AND HORROR

In 1993, Peter Hutchings proposed that horror is a genre generally perceived as being 'produced largely by men for a predominantly male audience and addressing specifically male fears and anxieties' (1993: 84). This abiding historical view of the genre as a distinctly "male" space[2], and the pervasiveness of certain ideas about women and their relationship to horror cinema, have been further inscribed into scholarship through several canonised pieces of work focusing on horror spectatorship.

Laura Mulvey (1975), for instance, presents the "gaze" considered typical of the thriller/horror genre as predominantly masculine in perspective, while Linda Williams stated that while 'little boys and grown men make it a point of honor' to watch horror unfold onscreen, 'little girls and grown women cover their eyes or hide behind the shoulders of their dates' (1983 [2015]: 17). This idea, that 'certain genres are, or ever have been, more "suitable" for women as either viewers or as filmmakers' (Cook, 2012: 38) is, obviously, unsound, as it presumes both a universality of experience and is shaded in assumptions based in gender essentialism. As Cynthia Freeland writes, 'these theories also standardly presume some connection between gazing, violent aggression, and masculinity', and that these are 'particular "male" motivations for making, watching and enjoying horror films' (1996: 195–196). Although women have always watched, been involved in, and created horror, it is true that even up until recently, as Tim Snelson advances, 'Film scholars continue to struggle in explaining the relationship between women and horror' and that most accounts 'rely on the assertion that the horror spectator is typically positioned as male and that the genre is founded upon the subjugation of women' (2014: 2). Thankfully, the cultural landscape is shifting, and scholarship such as *Phantom Ladies: Hollywood Horror and the Home Front* (Snelson, 2014) and *Women Make Horror: Filmmaking, Feminism, Genre* (Peirse, 2020a), women-centred festivals such as the Final Girls Berlin Film Festival, and several databases and websites like cuthroatwomen.org, have prompted debates around women and horror to move forward.

Stepping away from scholarship, this idea – that the horror genre is a space that is not for women as either creators or spectators – has also entered public consciousness through its repetition ad nauseum in popular journalism, such as Michelle Orange's thoughts on the popularity of the *Saw* franchise (2004–). After noting that both *Saw* (James Wan, 2004) and its 'torture porn kin' depict 'a steady stream of starlets being strung up, nailed down or splayed open', Orange presents her readers with a conundrum as to why 'recent box office receipts show that women have an even bigger appetite for these films than men. Theories straining to address this particular head scratcher have their work cut out for them: Are female fans of "Saw" ironists? Masochists? Or just dying to get closer to their dates?' (Orange, 2009).[3]

If women spectators of horror have confounded journalists such as Michelle Orange, one can only imagine how puzzled they would be by the presence of women in the industry and production of horror. More recently, there have been timely interventions in journalism highlighting the contributions of women to the genre, both as creators and audiences (see in particular Tyler (2019); Heller Nicholas (2018)). Despite this, it would seem that Orange does not stand alone in her assumptions, as can be discerned in the lived experiences of filmmakers such as Jennifer Kent and Sylvia Soska. While Kent recounts the surprise of acquaintances finding out she was directing a horror film, and that 'it was like I was directing a snuff film or porno or something terrible' (quoted in O'Sullivan, 2014), Soska commented that when she and her sister (and fellow filmmaker) Jen Soska tell people they direct horror, 'people would look at us and go, "Oh, honey, you don't have to do that." It was almost like they were talking about how I clean up roadkill for the city'. Soska remarks too that this was a response predicated on the 'preconceived notion that horror movies and women don't mix' (quoted in Wang, 2017), a view that can be traced back to Janet Maslin's damning statement that *The Slumber Party Massacre* (Amy Holden Jones, 1982) – a film both written and directed by women – is one of the more 'reprehensible' examples of slasher cinema, 'because its creators ought to know better' (Maslin, 1982).

While the flurry of attention that followed critically acclaimed horror films such as *A Girl Walks Home Alone at Night* (Ana Lily Amirpour, 2014), *The Babadook*, *The Invitation*, and *Raw* was both welcome and timely, it was not (and arguably, should not be expected to be) within the remit or responsibility of these journalistic articles to uncover the rich history of countless women who *have* found a space in horror, as fans, as scholars, and as creators. A broader ignorance of women's relationship with, and position within, the horror genre has not been helped by the lack of visibility that women have been offered historically. For example, despite the fact that a 1991 issue of *Fangoria* includes a few paragraphs on women and horror, written by then editor Tony Timpone, which declares 'It's time we put our sexist notions to bed and welcome the new voices in horror' (Timpone, 1991: 6), a year later they were still conspicuously absent. A reader's letter to the magazine in 1992 laments the lack of women in the "Fango Hall of Fame", and argues 'Come on, genre fans, there are many females who deserve the honor […] These women have done a lot for the genre […] Don't forget the women of the horror world' (Winkelman, 1992: 9). This demonstrates – despite the growing visibility of women working in horror afforded by recent developments – that there are, as Alison Peirse rightly points out, 'a vast number of women filmmakers completely absent from our written horror histories' (2020b: 10) and, until this is addressed, these histories continue to be incomplete.

'Soil's thin, but you'll manage': 1980s horror women and Mary, Queen of the Sematary

Before discussing Mary Lambert specifically, it is important to outline the genre context that she – as well as other women directors of the decade – were working within (and against), and outline some of the reasons why it was perceived to be a masculine space.

Horror is a genre that lends itself well to director-centred readings, both in journalism and in academia (with a commonality often being little in the way of deconstructing or questioning the concept of auteurism itself), but consideration as an 'auteur' or master of the genre is something that has traditionally been prohibited from women working within the genre. This can be seen in the *Masters of Horror* (Showtime, 2005–2007) anthology series, for instance, which ran for twenty-six episodes over two seasons and functioned to 'bestow prestige upon genre practitioners', while also asserting – quite clearly given the name of the series – that 'auteurship exists within horror cinema' (Kooyman, 2010: 198). It is telling then that this collection of filmmakers contained not a single woman until the series was rebranded as *Fear Itself* (NBC, 2008), which ran for one season and included Mary Harron's contribution of the episode "Community" (S01 E07).[4] As Joe Tompkins has argued, 'The notion that horror films merit serious critical attention is bound up with the proliferation of the concept of the horror auteur' (2014: 204), and this is a status that is bolstered by inclusion within such anthologies. George A. Romero, John Carpenter, Wes Craven, and David Cronenberg in particular were directors who had built their reputations within the genre during the 1970s, and were, as Peter Hutchings puts it, along with several other male directors, a set of 'customised "movie brats"' for the horror genre (2004: 181). By the mid-1980s at least, these directors had been canonised as the horror auteurs par excellence, and this status has since been cemented by various accolades, awards, and retrospectives. The masculinist concept of auteurism more broadly, and the prominence of these directors in the 1980s, may give the mistaken impression that horror was – to paraphrase the Peter Hutchings quote that opened this chapter – made by the boys, for the boys. Indeed, as I will explore below, Romero's status within the horror genre and his departure from the production of *Pet Sematary* – and particularly his replacement being a woman – did have some degree of impact on the film's reception.

In addition to the attention paid to these (male) directors in the 1980s (along with the impact of that into the 1990s and since) and their canonisation as horror auteurs, the decade's horror output is – as explored in Chapter Two – perceived as the golden era of slasher films, which are often categorised as being overarchingly misogynistic. Carol Clover, for example, notes that in the slasher film, although men may die too, women die precisely because they are female (1987 [2015]: 83) and that their death scenes, in contrast to male victims, are 'filmed at closer range, in more graphic detail, and at greater length' (1987 [2015]: 84). The consequent effect of this framing has been that slasher cinema has historically (rightly or wrongly) been perceived as serving male viewing pleasure and, as the 1980s is characterised as the golden age of this subgenre, the broader genre of horror in this decade is overarchingly perceived as being a space primarily for men. Additionally, a significant percentage of women working in front of the camera in 1980s horror, including Jamie Lee Curtis, Heather Langenkamp, Linnea Quigley, and Brinke Stevens were bestowed with the title of "Scream Queen". Barbara Crampton, in an incisive article entitled 'Don't Call Me A Scream Queen', argues that this term is both 'limiting in description and also limiting in its ability to reveal that these actresses are more than the sum of the strain of their vocal cords' (2016). The designation "Scream Queen" then suggests that these women's contributions to the horror genre are based solely on how well they scream and how attractive they might appear while doing so. As such, this diminishes the function of women in horror – and the varied and nuanced performances of these women – to set dressing for male audience enjoyment.

Essentially then, in the 1980s, these three elements – the canonisation of a new breed of male horror auteurs, the perception of 1980s horror as overtly misogynistic through the prominence of slashers, and the positioning of female bodies and screams as a novelty – betrays the fact that, as in previous decades, women were a distinct presence within the genre both as directors and in other creative roles. In addition to more "hidden" aspects of film production, such as assistant directing (Cindy Veazey for *Friday the 13th*), co-writing and producing (Debra Hill for *Halloween II* (Rick Rosenthal, 1981)), or casting (Annette Benson for *A Nightmare on Elm Street*), several women made their horror directorial mark in the 1980s. Along with lesser-known directors such as Beverley Sebastian (*Rocktober Blood* (1984)), Carol Frank (*Sorority House Massacre*

(1986)), and Kristine Peterson (*Deadly Dreams* (1988)), Oscar-winning director Kathryn Bigelow's second feature film, *Near Dark*, for example, mixed together the iconography of the western with the vampire film. Amy Holden Jones, in directing *Slumber Party Massacre* in 1982, sparked the first – and to date, only – slasher franchise to be helmed exclusively by women. Katt Shea's debut feature film, *Stripped to Kill* (1987), led to a sequel film, *Stripped to Kill 2: Live Girls*, which was, along with Shea's third horror feature, *Dance of the Damned*, released in 1989, and an overview of 1980s horror films directed by women would be incomplete without mentioning Jackie Kong's irreverent and gory entries in the genre, *The Being* (1983) and *Blood Diner* (1987). As is clear, women wanting to be involved with and create horror in the 1980s was not that unusual.

While Mary Lambert, born in Arkansas in 1951, would find her way to the horror genre late in the decade, she has stated that she felt – along with other filmmakers in the 1980s such as Kathryn Bigelow, Penelope Spheeris, and Martha Coolidge – that she was part of 'a little club of people that felt like nobody was going to hold us back' (quoted in Weiner, 2019). Before entering the world of feature films with her debut *Siesta*, Lambert had forged a successful path in directing music videos. Along with Janet Jackson's "Nasty", Lambert was perhaps best known for directing several of Madonna's early music videos, including the *Gentlemen Prefer Blondes* (Howard Hawks, 1953) homage of "Material Girl", the provocative "Like a Virgin", and "Like a Prayer". The video for "Like a Prayer" – which included stigmata, implied rape and murder, a field of burning crosses, and Madonna kissing a black saint-like figure on a Catholic altar – was met with a great deal of controversy. The Vatican condemned the video (Harrison, 2021), and it led to Madonna losing a lucrative advertising deal with the Pepsi company (Wollenberg, 1989). It would be only a mere month after this furore that *Pet Sematary* would be released.

Although Lambert would continue to direct music videos throughout the 1990s, working with Mötley Crüe, Queensrÿche, and the B-52's, among others, and did not initially position herself as a "horror director", her affinity for the genre has become clear through her repeated return to horror filmmaking since *Pet Sematary*. In addition to *Pet Sematary 2* (1992) – which I will examine in more depth in the following chapter – Lambert's horror output includes the campy teen thriller *The In Crowd* (2000), supernatural slasher *Urban Legends: Bloody Mary* (2005), psychological horror *The*

Attic (2007), and the monster romp *Mega Python vs. Gatoroid* (2011), along with the vampire-based web series *The Dark Path Chronicles* (2008–2009). Lambert has spoken several times about her desire to work more consistently in the horror genre, noting to journalist Simon Thompson that 'I have a big stack of horror movies that I have wanted to make in the 30 years, and they just haven't gotten made. People don't want to make them with me as the director' (quoted in Thompson, 2019). This statement seems to be supported by the fact that, in the years following *Pet Sematary*, Lambert's name has been attached to or considered for several horror projects that she ultimately did not get to direct, such as *Demon Knight* (Ernest Dickerson, 1995) and *The Gathering* (Brian Gilbert, 2006). She was also tipped to be a contributor to Brian Yuzna's *Deadly Sins* series, in which she was to direct the entry for the sin of pride (Ferrante, 1995: 8), but the series did not come to fruition. Other ultimately unmade projects include *In-Between*, which centred on cheating death ('The Terror Teletype', 1999: 9), and an adaptation of Robert R. McCammon's *Mine* (Shapiro, 1993: 10). The poor critical reception of *Pet Sematary 2* (stylised as *Pet Sematary Two*) – which is detailed in the following chapter – undoubtedly had an effect on the opportunities Lambert was offered through the 1990s and into the new millennium, leading her to state that, despite her success with *Pet Sematary* in 1989, 'I've had to fight every step of the way to be trusted with other horror movies [...] men are protecting what is seen as their territory and they don't want to give it up' (Thompson, 2019). Although paths into the horror genre are being forged for and by women then, there is clearly still a long road ahead.

It would seem that Mary Lambert, along with the many other women I have highlighted in this section, is doomed to have the prefix "woman" or "female" attached to her creative roles. Lambert herself has addressed this, noting that 'It's always a little annoying to be labelled a female film director because men are just "directors," then there's the double whammy of "female" horror director. How many boxes can you be put into?' (quoted in Marks, 2012). Even a decade and a half after the success of *Pet Sematary*, Stephen King was asked if 'a woman director brings a different sensibility to the film than a man would have' (Timpone, 2005: 68).[5] With this in mind, I should note that my intention throughout this chapter so far has not been, and is not, to present Lambert as a "feminine" filmmaker, or to imbue her work with any kind of reverent "womanliness". What I do argue, however, is that her gender did have an impact on her experiences directing *Pet Sematary* and the reportage of the production, particularly in light of George A. Romero's departure from the director's chair.

'IT'LL WORK THIS TIME': ADAPTING STEPHEN KING

In recent years the study of Stephen King adaptations has become a vibrant and growing area within the field of film studies. Along with Simon Brown's book *Screening Stephen King: Adaptation and the Horror Genre in Film and Television* (2018), there have also been various books dedicated to specific films such as *Carrie* (Mitchell, 2013), *The Shining* (Mee, 2017; Donnelly, 2018), and *Creepshow* (Brown, 2019). This being said, there has historically been a disproportionate amount of attention paid, both in scholarship and more broadly, to those King adaptations directed by individuals considered to be cinematic "auteurs". In a lot of these cases, I would follow Tony Magistrale in his argument that 'The reason for this, I suspect, has little to do with these films as adaptations of Stephen King novels and everything to do with the fact that Brian De Palma and Stanley Kubrick respectively directed them' (2003: xii).

Although obviously this is not the case with all work on *Carrie* and *The Shining*, with some accounts actively questioning the concept of auteurism, there is still a dominant auteurist focus within a good deal of the scholarship (and, indeed, fan and journalistic response) on these two films (see, for example Pezzotta, 2013; Keesey, 2015; and Bettinson, 2015), which looks at them more as examples of a particular director's style rather than adaptations of King's work. There is a converse scant amount of work on adaptations directed by those who have not received their "auteur" badge.

This deemphasis of *Carrie* and *The Shining* as "Stephen King films" may well be because they are both helmed by directors who have strong individualistic directorial styles that are easily discerned, such as the split screens of *Carrie* and the symmetry of *The Shining*. Another reason too may be because of a lack of King's involvement in their production, or – in the case of *The Shining* – his vocal contempt for the adaptation. Although based on his novels, neither *Carrie* nor *The Shining* feature a screenplay penned by King. *Carrie* – the first box-office success for De Palma – featured a screenplay by Laurence D. Cohen, who would go on to adapt several more King stories for the screen, including the miniseries for both *IT* (Tommy Lee Wallace, 1990) and *The Tommyknockers* (John

Power, 1993). The screenplay for *The Shining* meanwhile was created by Kubrick and Diana Johnson. In Laura Mee's superb analysis of the 1980 adaptation, she remarks on the copious notes that Kubrick and Johnson made on King's manuscript (housed in the Stanley Kubrick Archive at the University of the Arts in London), in which they make comments such as 'Do we need this? A good scene but what is the point?', and 'v. little plot in this chapter' (Mee, 2017: 41). Roger Luckhurst has noted that Kubrick and Johnson's screenplay 'clears the clutter' of the novel (Luckhurst, 2013: 38–39), but this focus on Kubrick's creative process and input into the story of *The Shining* has, as Mee argues, somewhat detached the film from its generic home of horror and instead reframed it as an example of Kubrick's auteurist vision (2017: 7). *The Shining* (1977) and *The Shining* (1980) operate as different entities, in particular from Stephen King's perspective it would seem, who in the foreword for the sequel novel to *The Shining*, *Doctor Sleep* (2013), stated:

> of course there was Stanley Kubrick's movie which many seem to remember – for reasons I have never quite understood – as one of the scariest films they have ever seen. If you have seen the movie but not read the novel, you should note that *Doctor Sleep* follows the latter which is, in my opinion, the True History of the Torrance Family.

Although some critics felt that Kubrick had improved King's story, such as Derek Malcolm, who bizarrely argues in his review of the film that the Stephen King narrative 'gets in the way of Kubrick's grim vision, finally cheapening and distorting it' (Malcolm, 1980), others have argued that King's dislike of the film stems from him appearing to be 'under the persistent misapprehension that Kubrick wanted to make a faithful adaptation of his novel' and his failure to realise that 'this was never Kubrick's intention' (Webster, 2011: 92).

There is a striking difference when we look at the relationship between Kubrick and his film's source novel and compare that to Mary Lambert's relationship with *Pet Sematary*. It has been widely observed that Lambert's film is considered one of the more 'faithful' adaptations of King's work, and Lambert herself has noted that she 'didn't come in with a vision of "How can we change this story to make it better? What can we do to solve the problems of this narrative?"' (quoted in Luers, 2016). Moreover, Lambert has expressed that her collaborative relationship with King was built on the fact that 'he sensed that I didn't want to change anything in his book, or put the emphasis in a different direction, but just bring [his] characters to life, bring that story to life, that family drama about obsession and death and where that leads' (quoted in Evangelista, 2019). The authorship of the filmic version of *Pet Sematary* therefore seems more equitable, with Stephen King providing the source material and the screenplay, and Mary Lambert contributing her own vision for the story and its characters.

Although King has maintained a general ambivalence towards cinematic adaptations of his work, noting that 'The movies have never been a big deal to me. The movies are the movies. They just make them. If they're good, that's terrific. If they're not, they're not' (quoted in Greene, 2014), certain adaptations, most notably *The Shining*, have drawn his ire. Perhaps because of his disappointment in Kubrick's film, the fact that his screenplays for both *Cujo* and *The Dead Zone* had been turned down (Brown, 2018: 97), and the poor critical reception of *Maximum Overdrive*, King created a list of conditions for the adaptation of *Pet Sematary* – a story he had an intense personal connection with. He insisted that the film was to be shot in Maine, that he would have final approval on the director, and that 'his script be used as written' (Brown, 2018: 97). Although I will not be engaging in any arbitrary difference spotting between the novel and the film, and the focus on fidelity as a measure of an adaptation's worth has, thankfully, been moved on from in adaptation studies, it is important to note here that in writing the screenplay for *Pet Sematary*, as he had done previously for *Creepshow*, *Cat's Eye*, *Silver Bullet*, and *Maximum Overdrive*, King was responsible for a large part of the adaptation process from book to screen. When any novel is adapted to film, this process necessitates some trimming down of the narrative as convoluted subplots are eliminated, flashback scenes removed or refigured, and characters shuffled around or taken out. There are certainly parts of the *Pet Sematary* source novel that did not make it into the screenplay, such as the overt presence of the Wendigo, several flashbacks exploring the animosity between Louis Creed and his father-in-law, Irwin Goldman, and a scattering of sex scenes. Other elements survive in different ways, such as the demise of Jud's wife, Norma, with Ellie Creed's first real encounter with death being changed to the death of Missy Dandridge, and the character of Norma being, instead, absent. Regardless of what was changed, when, and why, the impact of King being the screenwriter for *Pet Sematary* means that *he* made these decisions rather that someone else, which may have gone some way to explaining his positive commentary on the film.

It is no secret, as discussed in Chapter Three, that *Pet Sematary* is a book that Stephen King was reluctant to publish. In addition to his thoughts on the nihilistic outlook of the novel, *Pet Sematary* was also mythologised (and, indeed, advertised) as the work that had scared its own creator, with King noting that, if he had his way, the novel would 'still be in a drawer somewhere' (Breznican, 2019b). By 1984, a year after it was published, King had reportedly turned down several offers to sell the rights to make *Pet Sematary* into a film from 'almost every major studio', and also rejected 'a firm $1 million from a consortium' who wished to bring *Pet Sematary* to the screen (Harmetz, 1984). King would eventually sell the rights to Laurel Entertainment or, more specifically, to George A. Romero, 'for a handshake, a token payment of roughly $10,000, and a healthy share of any profits from the movie' (Harmetz, 1984). Although King had previously sworn that *Pet Sematary* would never be made into a film (Gross, 1986: 25), the reason for the selection of Romero as intended director was that, as King states in an interview from 1986, Romero 'knows how I feel about the book. I felt he could handle the subject better than anyone on earth' (quoted in Gross, 1986: 25). Romero and King had worked together previously on *Creepshow*,[6] and King had a small cameo in *Knightriders* (George A. Romero, 1981), so it seemed in 1984 that these two heavy hitters of horror would again be collaborating. But the road to filming *Pet Sematary* would be far more troubled.

'NOW I WANNA PLAY WITH YOU': THE PRODUCTION

Lindsay Doran had been advocating for a filmic adaptation of *Pet Sematary* since her time at Embassy Pictures in the early 1980s, and found when she moved to the position of vice-president of productions at Paramount that 'The prevailing opinion remained the same […] the time for Stephen King movies had come and gone' (Campopiano and White, 2017). However, the Writer's Guild of America strike in March to August of 1988 necessitated a need for studios to find scripts that needed no further writing work in order to fill their release schedule for 1989. Doran again pursued the idea of adapting *Pet Sematary*, a screenplay for which had already been written by Stephen King, and was given approval to obtain the rights. Although George A. Romero had been tipped as *Pet Sematary*'s director when the rights to the adaptation were bought by Laurel Entertainment in 1984, the sparse production slate at Paramount necessitated that *Pet Sematary* go into production almost immediately, with the intention being that the film would work for the studio as a 'quick and dirty exploitation' movie (King quoted in Wood, 1991: 39). Romero was, at the time, heavily involved with studio-mandated reshoots and post-production for *Monkey Shines* (George A. Romero, 1988) and, given the short lead time to begin production on *Pet Sematary*, had to turn the project down.

The news that Romero would not be directing *Pet Sematary* was quickly disseminated through outlets such as *Fangoria*, with an issue from 1988 declaring:

> The long-delayed movie version of Stephen King's *Pet Sematary* may finally go into production this year. Paramount Pictures acquired the option to distribute the King-scripted film from Laurel. That's the good news. The bad news is that George Romero may not be directing. A Laurel source reports that Mary Lambert, who directed the poorly-received *Siesta*, will helm.

(Timpone, 1988: 11)

This positioning, particularly within the pages of *Fangoria*, of Lambert as Romero's inexperienced and ill-suited foil, continued into reportage from the set during production. Issue 81 of *Fangoria* magazine in particular seems to fixate on the connection between Romero and *Pet Sematary*. The cover holds the tagline 'King's Pet Sematary: Where's Romero?', while the contents page makes it clear that Paramount's *Pet Sematary* is a 'Romeroless' King adaptation (1988: 5). The on-set report, compiled by Rodney A. Labbe, is more explicit in its comparison of Romero and Lambert, noting that the 'decidedly paranoid atmosphere' of the production, was underlined – he argues – by the fact that 'no amount of cajoling' could land him an interview with the director. Building on this, Labbe writes that an 'insider' on the set revealed to him that 'Mary wants to avoid controversy […] George Romero was supposed to direct *Pet Sematary*, and some people still think he ought to be doing it. She's understandably shaky about the assignment' (Labbe, 1988: 19), before noting Lambert's 'limited' experience in directing films. After *Pet Sematary*'s release, an interview conducted by Labbe with Ralph Singleton, who was – at the time – directing the adaptation of *Graveyard Shift* (1990), similarly details that Singleton was asked to attend the set of *Pet Sematary* during production in his function as associate producer, and as Singleton relates 'Mary Lambert, the director, was understandably a bit nervous about having me around' (Labbe, 1990: 33). Even years after the film, Labbe, in particular, seems to hold some kind of odd grudge against Lambert being chosen as the director of *Pet Sematary*, noting in a retrospective feature on the film that part of him 'itched' to find out 'what exactly gave her the edge' (2014: 18). Again, seemingly purely by dint of being a woman directing a horror feature for a major studio, Lambert's credentials had to be questioned.

Although reports such as those above underline Lambert's nervousness and inexperience, and even though King was a strong presence in the creative process and on set (the main filming location being in Ellsworth, not far from his home), the production of *Pet Sematary* was clearly a collaborative process. When asked in an interview in 1990 celebrating the "return" of Stephen King films to cinema (which *Pet Sematary* had no small part in heralding) what made him "accept" Lambert, 'an inexperienced director with only one poorly received film' as the director for *Pet Sematary*, King responds how 'excited' he was by *Siesta*, and that he believed Lambert to be 'somebody who has a lot of guts' (quoted in Nutman, 1990: 26). This response is characteristic of King's clear support of Lambert, both at the time of the production and in the years after. For example, in a retrospective article on the film from 2019 – a few weeks prior to the release of the remake – King notes that 'Mary Lambert came on board. I really liked her. I thought that she was cool and had good ideas about it. Also, I wanted to be Mary's advocate on it' (quoted in Breznican, 2019a). Lambert herself has referred to King as her 'ally' during the production (quoted in Breznican, 2019b).

Special effects makeup artist Lance Anderson noted that watching King collaborate with Lambert was 'fun', and that King 'wasn't trying to push his ideas. In fact, […] he actually liked the changes made […] he endorsed them' (Campopiano and White, 2017). Lambert has spoken several times about the amiable working relationship between herself and King, stating that she 'had a lot of ideas about how to tell the story visually [...] and some of those things involved little changes within scenes [...] I was never afraid or had any problems calling Stephen up and saying, "I have an idea" or "What if we do it like this"' (Weiner, 2019).

Lambert affirmed in another interview that King would often reply to the effect of '"Yeah, that's a great idea. And then...", and he'd always put another cherry on top. [He'd] be like "Yes, and then we'll do that, and then we'll really scare them!"' (Evangelista, 2019). Additionally, King has repeatedly noted how Lambert's directorial choices improved the story. In the script for *Pet Sematary*, for example, the fight scene between Jud and the Gage-creature is accompanied by a note that says 'This one's got to be pretty rough. George will know what to do'. Some fifteen years after the film's release, King stated:

> it was my idea that the dead child should be under the bed, because we know in our secret fears that the bad thing is always waiting for us there. But it was Mary who came up with the idea that the kid would use the scalpel to slice Jud's Achilles' tendon.
>
> (Timpone, 2005: 68) (see Figure 17)

The tendon injury has been repeatedly used in horror cinema since.[7] Clearly, Mary knew 'what to do', and how to do a Stephen King film right too.

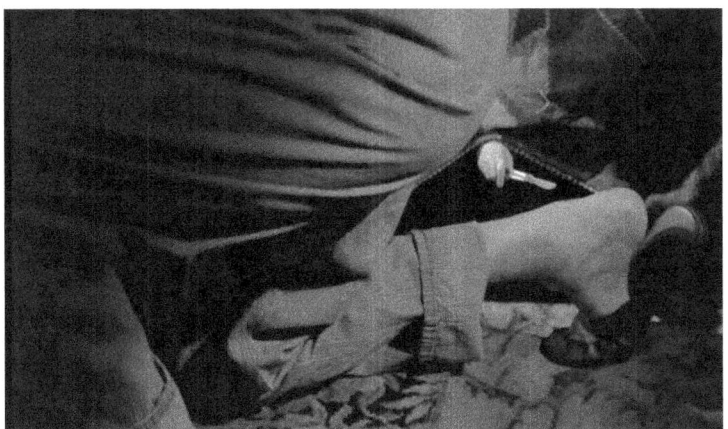

Figure 17. Always look under the bed for scalpel wielding toddlers

Among the many aspects of the film that show Lambert's directorial stamp, the influence of her background as an artist can be seen in the expressionist way that both Missy's death scene and Rachel's ascent up the staircase in Jud's house are filmed (see Figure 18). Both scenes are filled with shadows, sharp angles jut in at the characters, and in some frames the camera is canted in a disorientating way. Lambert has also spoken multiple times regarding how folklore influences her choices in directing, and *Pet Sematary* – like *Siesta*, *Urban Legend: Bloody Mary*, and *The Attic* – carry her signature style in terms of themes: obsession, death, secrets, dark magic, and form: with dream sequences, strong visual symbolism, and flashback scenes.

Figure 18. The expressionistic influence within Pet Sematary

The archetypal quality of the story was an element Lambert wanted to thread through the casting too, with Dale Midkiff as Louis being 'just the classic young professional' and Denise Crosby and Blaze Berdahl[8] being cast to complete the all-American family. Along with casting director Fern Champion, Lambert found she had to lobby Paramount for both Miko Hughes as Gage Creed, due to an industry preference in casting twins in the part of young children due to child labour laws, and Fred Gwynne as Jud, who Paramount were against casting due to his previous work in comedy as Herman Munster within *The Munsters* (CBC, 1964–1966). Rather than being the inexperienced and nervous character she is painted as in Labbe's reportage from the set, it would seem that Mary Lambert entered the *Pet Sematary* project with a clear vision in mind and, in collaborating closely with King, created a film that put cinematic adaptations of King's work back in favour.

The premiere of *Pet Sematary* was held in New York – with an advance screening in Bangor, Maine – after which the film reached blockbuster level, grossing $12 million on its opening weekend (Hughes, 1990: 11), and topping the box-office chart for three weeks (Easton, 1989). The total US domestic gross for the film was $57,469,179, with a home video gross of £26,400,000. *Pet Sematary*, at the time of its release, stood as the most profitable Stephen King adaptation to date, and would hold that position until the release of *Misery* (Rob Reiner, 1990). Producer Richard P. Rubenstein commented that he was 'particularly surprised and impressed by the age range of the audience, and by the above-average number of women going to see the picture' (Hughes, 1990: 12), with the latter being a demographic that was key to the film's success. Despite the fact that, in a retrospective on *Pet Sematary*, Rodney A. Labbe noted a crew member on the set had remarked to him that 'The shadow of Romero is hanging over us like a shroud' (2014: 18), and although the film received mixed reviews, Lambert's direction was singled out in several of these for praise. Philip Strick, for instance, noted that Lambert 'falls on King's story with an enjoyable ferocity [and] expands the formulaic horror into something modestly more substantial by maintaining a furious pace and a grip that knows when to relax' (1989: 342). Lambert has stated since the film's release that 'Honestly, I don't think people thought it was going to be as successful as it was', before wondering if *Pet Sematary* essentially 'slipped through the cracks' due to the fact that '[King] had other projects with Paramount that had other writers and bigger, more important directors than myself, bigger stars, whatever' (Evangelista, 2019). The success of the film, however, not only gave Hollywood 'a great deal more confidence in the horror film' (Rubenstein quoted in Hughes, 1990: 13) but, as Simon Brown rightly notes, 'thanks to *Pet Sematary*, the cinematic Brand Stephen King had regained cultural capital' (Brown, 2018: 102). *Pet Sematary* would go on to become the highest grossing horror film of 1989, and – at the time of writing – remains the highest grossing horror film directed by a woman in cinematic history. The film led to the recalibration of Stephen King properties, which 'reacquired both cultural capital and box-office potential' (Brown, 2018: 96), a re-evaluation bolstered the following year with the release of *Misery*, the only Stephen King adaptation to date to win an Academy Award, for Kathy Bates as Best Actress.[9]

So far seemingly overlooked in horror scholarship, Mary Lambert helmed *Pet Sematary* in an era of horror cinema that has been historically perceived as offering entertainment to a predominantly male audience. However, assumptions around horror spectatorship and the suitability of the genre as a space for women – both as audiences and creators – are clearly unfounded. Despite this, it would be naïve to state that Lambert – as a woman directing a film written by a popular horror author on a production that had seen the recent departure of a well-respected male director colleague – did not face unique challenges and reportage on her film that felt distinctly gendered. Although Lambert may never (and is not required to) be canonised as a master of horror, she collaborated with King to produce a film that aligned with her own stylistic tendencies and thematic interests as a director, and one which resonated with the audiences of the time. *Pet Sematary* stands then not only as a key turning point in the fortunes of the Stephen King brand, but a crucial entry in 1980s horror cinema, with the success of *Pet Sematary* meaning that the decade of King closed on an upward swing and, as the chapter that follows demonstrates, left a long-lasting legacy.

Notes

1. This club is reported to be extending to three members soon, with Lynne Ramsey announced as the director of a cinematic adaptation of *The Girl Who Loved Tom Gordon* (1999) (Kit, 2020).
2. Along with horror, Pam Cook notes that the western and the gangster film are two other genres perceived as being "masculine" (2012: 31).
3. This view, that "torture porn" is misogynistic is dispelled by Steve Jones who, in a survey of forty-five films belonging to the subgenre, found that the ratio of men killed to women was 244 to 108 (with an additional 293 incidences of serious injury committed on a male body to 144 incidences of comparable injuries to women (2013: 133).
4. The gender balance in various subsequent anthology collections is comparable. In the films *The ABCs of Death* (Various, 2012) and *The ABCs of Death 2* (Various, 2014) for instance, of the fifty-two possible directorial slots, only four are occupied by women. Similarly, in the first three *V/H/S* films, women are absent again. Although the more recent *V/H/S/94* (Various, 2021) and *V/H/S/99* (Various, 2022) do include four contributions – out of ten – from women directors. The *Tales from the Crypt* series (HBO, 1989–1996) has three episodes out of a possible ninety-three being directed by women – one of which, "Collection Completed" (S01 E06), is by Mary Lambert. More recently, *Creepshow* (Shudder, 2019–) has thus far fared (only slightly) better, with two segments from Roxanne Benjamin, and two from Axelle Carolyn, of a possible thirty-three segments over seventeen episodes. The broader and evident exclusion of women

creators was said by writer-director Jovanka Vuckovic to be the impetus behind the creation of the all-women anthology film *XX* (Various, 2017), which was made as 'a direct response to the lack of opportunities for women in the horror genre in particular' (quoted in Galuppo, 2017). It is important to note too that the majority of women who have been included in these anthologies are white and cisgender, demonstrating a need for further diversity and inclusion.

5. King, to his credit, responded that 'The answer is a resounding "no." […] it's as tough as it needs to be in the Mary Lambert version. Other than if it had been directed by the ghost of Sam Peckinpah, I can't imagine it being any harder or harder-edged than it is now' (quoted in Timpone, 2005: 68).

6. Outside of collaborations, King and Romero also maintained a personal friendship. The strength of this shown when George A. Romero died in 2017, and King tweeted 'Sad to hear my favourite collaborator – and good old friend – George Romero has died. George, there will never be another like you' (King, 2017).

7. To be clear, I am not arguing that Lambert was the first to include an Achilles tendon slice in horror cinema; the scene in *Pet Sematary* is, I argue, a clear inspiration for similar scenes in *Urban Legend* (Jamie Blanks, 1998), *Hostel* (Eli Roth, 2005), and *House of Wax* (Jaume Collet-Serra, 2005) to name only a few subsequent films.

8. Although Blaze Berdahl is listed as portraying Ellie Creed in the film's credits, she shared the role with her twin sister, Beau Berdahl.

9. Although *Carrie* was nominated in two categories in 1977, *Stand By Me* in one category in 1987, *The Shawshank Redemption* (Frank Darabont, 1994) in seven categories in 1995 and *The Green Mile* (Frank Darabont, 1999) for four in 2000, none of these films won an award in any category.

Chapter 5: 'Sometimes dead is better' (?): revisiting and remaking Stephen King and *Pet Sematary*

It would be fair to say that sequels and remakes – two modes of production that Thomas Leitch describes as 'cousins' (2001: 41) – have often been disparaged in horror history, despite playing 'a major role in the horror movie from cinema's inception' (Jess-Cooke, 2009: 55). Sequels and remakes are frequently positioned as media products that act as a 'textual leech, a formulaic financial format, and the assassin of "originality"' (Jess-Cooke and Verevis, 2010: 4) in addition to, as detailed below, greedy money-grabs.

This chapter will begin to explore the legacy of *Pet Sematary* through first examining its sequel, *Pet Sematary 2*, and how this film ties itself firmly to the original, before moving on to examine the King Renaissance of 2017. The remake of *Pet Sematary* in 2019 will then be explored as an adaptation that is situated firmly within an era of nostalgia for past decades of horror cinema, despite its own lack of nostalgia for the previous cinematic iteration of the story. I will draw attention in the latter part of this chapter to various questions that can be asked concerning remakes: how do they allow us to revisit and re-evaluate previous films? And, more specifically to this book, what positions do *Pet Sematary* (1989) and *Pet Sematary* (2019) occupy in the broader corpus of Stephen King adaptations? Finally, I will examine the connective tissues between these two versions of the story, and how these connections are severed or used to bind the two films together.

'I know your dog died, but get a grip': revisiting the deadfall in *Pet Sematary 2*

If we are to take an overview of North American horror films released in 1989, at first glance Richard P. Rubenstein's assertion that the genre was full of 'sequels and rehashes' (Szebin, 1989a: 6) seems to be accurate. These included *Halloween 5: The Revenge of Michael Myers* (Dominique Othenin-Girard), *Friday the 13th Part VIII: Jason Takes Manhattan* (Rob Hedden), and *A Nightmare on Elm Street 5: The Dream Child* (Stephen Hopkins), with each of these being the poorest performing instalments of their respective franchises. Direct-to-video or television sequels such as *Amityville 4: The Evil Escapes* (Sandor Stern) and *Howling V: The Rebirth* (Neal Sandstrom) were also released to negative receptions. Given how financially successful *Pet Sematary* was, it comes as no surprise that a sequel film was green lit shortly after its release.

Alongside the many direct adaptations of Stephen King's work since 1976, there are also a variety of films and television series that are inspired by, derived from, or act as unofficial sequels to these adaptations.[1] Throughout the 1990s in particular there was a steady stream of King sequels and spinoffs such as *Lawnmower Man: Beyond Cyberspace* (Farhad Mann, 1996), *Sometimes They Come Back… Again* (Adam Grossman, 1996), *Sometimes They Come Back… For More* (Daniel Zelik Berk, 1998), and *The Rage: Carrie 2* (Katt Shea, 1999). 1984's *Children of the Corn* provided particularly fruitful ground for follow-up films, inspiring no less than four sequels in the 1990s alone.[2] The following section will speak to the clear renaissance of all things King-tinged in the 2010s, but first I wish to trace this thirst for King derivatives back to its beginning.

The first film derived from a Stephen King adaptation was *A Return to 'Salem's Lot* (Larry Cohen, 1987), a sequel to *'Salem's Lot* (Tobe Hooper, 1979), the positively received CBS miniseries. This was, however, a cinematic sequel to a televisual adaptation. The first film-to-film sequel is *Pet Sematary 2*, released in August 1992. With no surviving characters from the original film returning, *Pet Sematary 2* starred Edward Furlong – who had recently found stardom in another sequel, *Terminator 2: Judgement Day* (James Cameron, 1991) – in the role of protagonist, Jeff Matthews. Along with Furlong, *Pet Sematary 2* features a pre-*ER* (NBC, 1994–2009) Anthony Edwards, best known at this point for his role as Goose in *Top Gun* (Tony Scott, 1986) playing Jeff's father Chase, and Clancy Brown of *Highlander* (Russell Mulcahy, 1986) and *Blue Steel* (Kathryn Bigelow, 1990) in the role of primary antagonist, Gus.

Pet Sematary 2 opens with the death of Renee Hallow (Darlanne Fluegel), an actress who is electrocuted in an accident on the set of her new horror film. Her son Jeff and estranged husband Chase move back to Renee's hometown in Ludlow, Maine, shortly after her funeral. Jeff makes fast friends with a local boy, Drew (Jason McGuire), who has a dog called Zowie. He is also quick to make an adversary in Clyde (Jared Rushton), the local bully. After Zowie is shot by Gus, Drew's antagonistic stepfather and town sheriff, Drew asks Jeff to help him bury his pet, and takes him to the Micmac burial ground. After Zowie is buried, he returns to Drew. A few days later, Gus crashes a gathering of local kids – including Jeff and Drew – at Halloween; he is fatally mauled by Zowie and Jeff and Drew decide (of course) to bury him in the Micmac ground too. Gus returns and, although initially Drew remarks that 'it's like he forgot he hates me', he quickly becomes increasingly violent and erratic. Gus kills Clyde after happening upon a fight between him and Jeff, and then pursues and kills Drew, who witnessed Clyde's murder, along with Drew's mother, Amanda (Lisa Waltz). Jeff, who becomes increasingly withdrawn after Drew's funeral, decides to reanimate Renee and is assisted by Gus, who exhumes her body. Chase becomes aware of this exhumation and rushes to Drew's house where he fights with and kills both Zowie and Gus. Returning home, Chase finds his housekeeper murdered, and Jeff and Renee embracing in the attic, where Jeff has recreated his mother's dressing room. A reanimated Clyde then knocks out Chase and fights with Jeff, who eventually defeats Clyde and breaks down the door. Renee implores Jeff to stay and join her in death as her face begins to melt, revealing the injuries sustained in her accident. As Renee shrieks 'Stay with me! Dead is Better!' Jeff leaves with his father. The final scene shows Jeff and Chase locking the veterinary clinic where Chase worked, and driving away from Ludlow.

Carolyn Jess-Cooke and Constantine Verevis have proposed that, unlike remakes, 'the sequel does not prioritize the repetition of an original, but rather advances an exploration of alternatives, differences, and reenactments that are discretely charged with the various ways in which we may reread, remember, or return to a source' (2010: 5). In this way, *Pet Sematary 2* serves its purpose well; it explores alternatives by centring on different families – the Creeds vs. the Matthews – and differences by featuring a reanimated dog instead of a reanimated cat. It also re-enacts the emotional breakdown of Louis Creed through the breakdown of Jeff Matthews. And, as is perhaps expected from a sequel, it returns to the original film several times with multiple visual and narrative references. Carolyn Jess-Cooke has suggested that 'the sequel effectively markets, interprets, substantiates and re-identifies generic cues, texts and origins, thereby promising a much more participatory experience' (2009: 53), and it could be argued that spotting these references to the first film are part of a participatory experience for a viewer familiar with it. Aside from the obvious visual presence of the pet cemetery and the Micmac burial ground, the Creed house features prominently in two shots early in the film. First, when Clyde and his gang ride past the house on their bicycles, and then again as Jeff rides past in his chase of them.[3] The mailbox, with 'CREED' clearly marked on the side, is closer in this second shot – seemingly to give the audience two chances to pick up the reference (see Figure 19). This is perhaps one of the most clear and prominent visual references to *Pet Sematary* contained in the sequel, but there are several references in the dialogue too.

Figure 19. Pet Sematary 2 ties itself visually to the original film

Clyde and his gang, for instance, mention the 'Creed Murders' in their first confrontation with Jeff, and this is then expanded on during the Halloween gathering, when Clyde recounts:

> That old Louis was one sick puppy. Digging up little Gage, maggots pouring out of the dead kid's eyes. Ellie Creed was the only one that lived, then one night she freaks out, hacks up the grandparents with an axe. Police found her licking the brains off the blade. Threw her in the psycho ward, all she could say were two words: "Pet Sematary". Here's the best part, two nights ago she escaped. Man, I hope she doesn't show up here. We wouldn't even recognise her, not if she was wearing a costume. She could be one of us …

Although Clyde's antics are cut short by the arrival of Gus, it is clear that the characters in *Pet Sematary 2* engage with the Creed Murders as a kind of urban legend or, as Drew puts it, 'Just an old ghost story', despite the murders taking place narratively only a few years prior. The character of Quentin Yolander (Jim Peck) too, Chase's predecessor at the veterinary clinic, is a key connection between the two films. While Zowie is under the care of Chase, he sends off bloodwork to the pathologist who, when he calls back, asks if it is Chase's idea of a joke to send blood from a dead animal. Met with confusion and bemusement from Chase, the pathologist notes that the last person who did that was Yolander, prompting Chase to trace Ludlow's previous vet down. After a short conversation about 'the Creed cat', Yolander confirms that 'There's no blood condition, the dog isn't sick, it's dead. And so was Creed's cat, and so was his wife on the night she was killed for the second time'. Leitch states that sequels and remakes have fundamentally different appeals, and that, with sequels, the audience 'wants to find out more, to spend more time with characters they are interested in and to find out what happened to them after their story was over' (2001: 44). Unfortunately, despite Clyde's horror story about Ellie, and Yolander's brief mention of the fate of Rachel Creed, the audience are never given a definitive answer on what happened to Ellie Creed after the deaths of her family, a story that Mary Lambert wanted to continue.

In the years following *Pet Sematary 2*'s release, Lambert has been candid in discussions about the film, and clear that the storyline was not the one she initially wanted to explore. Speaking in 2019, Lambert explicitly stated that she wanted to directly continue the story of the first film, with the focus on a now teenaged Ellie Creed returning to Ludlow. Lambert lamented however:

> It was a time in history when it was – not too long ago – where it was kind of felt that women couldn't carry a movie, and especially a young girl couldn't carry a movie and that it wasn't such a good idea to do a sequel with Ellie as the main protagonist […] I don't know that [it] was actually voiced by anybody, but nobody wanted to make a sequel with Ellie as the protagonist.
>
> (quoted in Evangelista, 2019)

Lambert expanded on this during another interview from around this time, explaining that she still wanted to make a sequel to *Pet Sematary* and that 'I had this whole idea, because I love cats, that there would be a community of feral cats there, and the community wanted to get rid of the feral cats [...] Then, actually, the feral cats would lead [Ellie] to her father in some way' (quoted in Breznican, 2019b). Although Lambert clearly enjoys explaining her original ideas for the *Pet Sematary* sequel with various interviewers, she also commented, rather more sombrely, that 'My career is really littered with the projects I wanted to do that were about women' and that 'They all got thrown back at me because most of the time it was like "We can't do this with a female protagonist"' (quoted in Yamato, 2019). Lambert has expressed regret at not being able to continue her time with the Creeds, and is evidently still interested in the story, as seen in her aside that 'if any serious producers want to hear my idea for a sequel, I'd be happy to tell them. It would be a true sequel, not a remake!' (quoted in Luers, 2016). It is intriguing too that Lambert does not really count *Pet Sematary 2* as a sequel, but instead as 'another story about the Pet Sematary, basically' (Wojnar, 2019).

Lambert has argued that *Pet Sematary 2* stands as a more irreverent take on the story, and that she wanted 'to get into the idea of what goes on in a teenage boy's head. Why do they do stupid things?' (quoted in Luers, 2016). Lambert's second *Pet Sematary* film is, in many ways, harsher than the original. The soundtrack, for example, is full of contemporaneous alternative rock bands and this is of course a continuation of the inclusion of The Ramones in the first film. The songs featured in the second film, however, such as L7's "Shit List" and The Nymphs' "Revolt" have a noticeably harder edge.[4] *Pet Sematary 2* feels – for want of a better word – more spiteful. The gore is noticeably increased, with graphic depictions of rabbits being skinned, the remains of kittens who have been mauled and partially eaten, and oozing, bloody, wounds. Whereas in *Pet Sematary* the person-on-person violence is limited to Timmy Baterman dragging his father back into a house fire, and injuries to Jud, Rachel, and Louis at the hands of Gage, *Pet Sematary 2* features a litany of violent acts and aftermaths. These include: a sexual assault; a teenager having his face ripped off by a motorcycle wheel; a drill exploring a shoulder wound; a close-range head shot; and a thumb being forced into an eye. Mary Lambert's gore and horror credentials – which were called into question during the production of the first film – are emphatically underlined in *Pet Sematary 2*, with the increase in violence seemingly being at Lambert's behest, as she noted that what attracted her to helm the sequel film is that 'I could bring some of my own taste, feeling and story ideas' (Nicoll, 1992: 47). Unfortunately, however, reports on the production of the film in *Fangoria* seemed more interested in Lambert's status as a pregnant woman than in her directorial skill. An on-set report by Gregory Nicoll, for example, notes that Lambert's voice has an 'unmistakably motherly tone' as she speaks to Edward Furlong (Nicoll, 1992: 46), and describes her physical appearance three times within four pages.

Stephen King, one of the loudest supporters of the original *Pet Sematary* film, was less kind in his thoughts on the sequel and, in an interview with *Fangoria* around the time of the film's production, stated:

> The sequel has now been made. I read the script – or as much of it as I could stand – and I read enough to realize that it was exactly like the first Pet Sematary with different characters. I don't approve of this movie and I didn't want it made. I hope that the people who read Fangoria, the people who read my books and who like my stuff will stay away from this picture. And this is one that I will not see myself.
>
> (quoted in Stroby, 1992: 30)

Although it is doubtful whether King's strongly worded plea to the readers of *Fangoria* had much of an effect on the reception of *Pet Sematary 2*, it did perform relatively disappointingly compared to the success of the original film, grossing $17.1 million to its $8 million budget. It has also been largely absent from horror studies scholarship – with a notable exception being Douglas Keesey's (2018) enlightening analysis of the film's broader themes, in which he re-evaluates its contribution to the horror genre. As time has moved on, however, it has been the subject of several nostalgic retrospective pieces (such as Navarro (2017); Harber (2019)). King's approval was sought – and gained – for the next visitation to the Micmac burial ground in the 2019 remake. Before I move on to discuss this later incarnation of the story, however, it is important to lay out the context it emerged from – a context quite different from that of the original film – where the cultural capital of the Stephen King brand was again on the rise.

'Remember, doc': rose-tinted screams and Stephen King in an age of nostalgia horror

As Kayla McCarthy argues, the 2010s saw a 'significant increase in American media that takes people back to the recent past through nostalgia' (2019: 663). Although present in varied media products, this nostalgia can be seen manifesting in multiple ways within the horror genre. Predated by the Robert Rodriguez and Quentin Tarantino helmed double bill *Grindhouse* (2007), which sought to recreate the visual experience of 1970s exploitation cinema, the release of *The House of the Devil* (Ti West, 2009) heralded an ongoing strand of horror media that I will classify as 'nostalgia horror': a rough grouping of films, television shows, and other media that use 1980s (and early 1990s) horror specifically as their aesthetic and cultural reference point. Nostalgia horror includes films such as *Beyond the Black Rainbow* (Panos Cosmatos, 2010), *Paranormal Activity 3* (Henry Joost and Ariel Schulman, 2011), *You're Next* (Adam Wingard, 2011), *WNUF Halloween Special* (Chris LaMartina, 2013), *Almost Human* (Joe Begos, 2014), *It Follows* (David Robert Mitchell, 2014), *The Guest* (Adam Wingard, 2014), *The Final Girls*, *The Void*, *Beyond the Gates* (Jackson Stewart, 2016), *Summer of '84* (Anouk Whissell, François Simard, and Yoann-Karl Whissell, 2018), *The Ranger* (Jennifer Wexler, 2018), *Color Out of Space* (Richard Stanley, 2019), *VFW* (Joe Begos, 2019), *Rent-a-Pal* (Jon Stevenson, 2020) *Vicious Fun* (Cody Calahan, 2020), and *V/H/S:94* (Various, 2021); television programmes like *American Horror Story: 1984* (FX, 2019), *The Haunting of Bly Manor* (Netflix, 2019), and *Archive 81* (Netflix, 2022), as well as the podcast *Video Palace* (Ben Rock, 2018). These narratives range from clear homages to horror entries from specific decades and period pieces, to the use of 1980s style practical effects, or mediations on the tropes, conventions, and media formats of the past. Two pieces of media in particular, however – the strongly Stephen King flavoured Netflix original series *Stranger Things* (Netflix, 2016–) and the remake of *It* (in the renamed *It: Chapter One* (Andy Muschietti, 2017)) – have found extraordinary success.

Stranger Things was released on the streaming service Netflix in 2016, and quickly became one of the providers most successful original series, drawing 8.2 million viewers in its first sixteen days (Miller, 2016). Although not based on a Stephen King story, the series uses King's narratives as inspiration. This element of the show was noticed immediately by critics, such as Hadley Freeman's assessment of the first season, when she explains that *Stranger Things* 'took the camaraderie of Stand By Me […] and sci-fi of Firestarter' (Freeman, 2017) to create a 1980s period piece. Indeed, King's work is heavily and often directly referenced in the show itself, with multiple scenes taking visual cues from several cinematic King adaptations. King himself tweeted of the show that watching it was like watching 'Steve King's Greatest Hits. I mean that in a good way' (King, 2016), and the pointed line in the sixth episode of the first season, where two of the main characters are asked 'Do you read any Stephen King?' makes it clear that the author's work is part of the DNA of *Stranger Things*.[5] The show's creators, twin brother team Matt and Ross Duffer, have been completely open about the strong King influence on the series, noting for example that the show's distinctive title font was inspired by 1980s Stephen King paperback covers and, in pitching the series to different networks, 'we made a little look book […] we made it look like an old Stephen King book' (Fienberg, 2016). *Stranger Things* was a pop culture phenomenon, with various outlets claiming that the show was an example of how to do nostalgia 'right'. The clear visual and narrative similarities to Stephen King works and adaptations within *Stranger Things* would bolster King's cultural capital, and further situate King's name and distinct brand of horror as central to conceptions of the 1980s.

The release of *It: Chapter One*, as the first of a two-part feature film adaptation of King's 1986 novel, solidified the connection between nostalgia horror and Stephen King. The narrative in both *It: Chapter One* and *It: Chapter Two* (Andy Muschietti, 2019) is updated from its original 1950s and 1980s setting – reflecting when the group of characters were children and adults – to a comparable 1980s and 2010s timeframe and, just as the novel could be seen as 'a museum filled with the popular culture of the 1950s: brand names, rock 'n' roll songs and stars, the jokes and routines of childhood in that era' (Lehman-Haupt, 1986), Andy Muschietti's films are similarly imbued with a nostalgia for the 1980s. References include repeated lines regarding New Kids on the Block, a cinema marquee advertising *A Nightmare on Elm Street 5: The Dream Child*, and 1980s fashions (including a particularly heinous mullet on bully Henry Bowers). Although these are perhaps more subtle than the visual cues in *Stranger Things*,[6] the similarities between *Stranger Things* and *It* in an age of broader 1980s nostalgia of course invited comparison, and lent commentary on the two *It* films a curious tone. *It* (the novel) is one of the strongest of the Stephen King influences on the first season of *Stranger Things*, given that it is about a group of pre-teens that travel primarily by bicycle and fight a being from a different reality. Just as the group of 'Losers' in *It* contain a lone female, Beverly Marsh, El of *Stranger Things* is similarly the only girl in a group of boys.[7] Shades of the psychotic Henry Bowers can be found in the characterisation of Troy, who threatens to cut the character of Dustin similarly to how Henry cut Ben Hanscom, and just as Pennywise appears to the Losers in the form of various 1950s horror monsters such as the werewolf, the gang in *Stranger Things* make sense of the creature in their narrative through their knowledge of "Dungeons and Dragons", a popular board game in the 1980s. It is curious, therefore, that *Stranger Things* then became a key comparison point for *It: Chapter One*, a film adaptation of a novel that predates *Stranger Things* by thirty years.

Just as *Pet Sematary* reinvigorated the cinematic Stephen King brand for the 1990s, the success of the *It* films has made Stephen King adaptations hot property in Hollywood for the 2020s. The trend towards works inspired by or derivative of Stephen King works continues and, along with prequel *Children of the Corn* (Kurt Wimmer, 2020), there are more explicit and direct references to King's work contained in *Castle Rock* (Hulu, 2018–2019). The forthcoming series *Overlook* too will focus on the untold stories from the hotel at the centre of *The Shining* (Andreeva, 2021). Adaptations of *The Breathing Method* (1982) and *The Long Walk* (1979) among others have all been confirmed to be in planning or production stages.[8] This is in addition to remakes of previously adapted works, such as *Firestarter* (Keith Thomas, 2022), and *'Salem's Lot* (Gary Dauberman, 2023).[9] The first remake to be released cinematically in the wake of *It: Chapter One*, however, was the remake/readaptation of *Pet Sematary*.

'YOU MAKE UP THE SWEETEST SMELLING REASONS TO GO BACK': *PET SEMATARY* (2019)

As Laura Mee has previously stated, 'Remakes are often framed as a particularly low form of adaptation, and so the horror remake is arguably seen as the lowest of the low' (Mee, 2022: 26). There are several reasons for this, such as the erroneous idea that a remake somehow erases or pays disrespect to an original film purely by dint of existing. Remakes have also been positioned as lazy cash-grabs that function to squeeze more money out of audiences, with nothing being 'safe' from 'the greedy hands of studio executives' (Hantke, 2010: 10). Moreover, the prominence of remakes in the early years of the twenty-first century – particularly those produced by Platinum Dunes – led to them being situated as a sign that the genre as it stood at the beginning of the millennium was creatively exhausted.[10] The most often cited criticism of remakes, however, is their apparent "pointlessness".

Taking a mercenary perspective for a moment, if we cynically accept that the intention of remakes is to make more money from a pre-sold property, then *Pet Sematary*, considering how well it did financially, is a sensible film to select for remaking. Despite its financial success, however, *Pet Sematary* has never been placed on the same pedestal that its adaptation contemporaries such as *Carrie* or *The Shining* have. This is particularly apparent in a review of *Pet Sematary* 2019 which states that the makers of the film have an advantage, given that 'they don't have a *true classic* along the lines of Brian De Palma's "Carrie" or Stanley Kubrick's "The Shining" casting a shadow over their efforts' and that 'all they really have to do is come up with something marginally better than an unforgivably terrible movie' (Sobczynski, 2019, emphasis added). This works in favour of a remake, because – as James Naremore states – remakes 'are in danger of being assigned a low cultural status, or even of eliciting critical opprobrium, because they are copies of "culturally treasured" originals' (2000: 12). It follows, then, that if *Pet Sematary* is not culturally treasured, then the possibility of a remake eliciting this revile is distinctly lessened.

The original *Pet Sematary*'s reception was characterised by mixed to negative reviews, with the latter of these calling it – among other things – 'sickening' (Siskel, 1989), 'wholly devoid of atmosphere and nuance' (Kehr, 1989), and 'undead schlock dulled by a slasher-film mentality' (Variety Staff, 1989). It is fair to say then, that at the time of its release and in the years following, *Pet Sematary* was not really considered a key – or 'culturally treasured' – King adaptation, with the film further tarnished by the release of what many saw as a sub-par sequel. The reviews for *Pet Sematary* 2019 – like its predecessor – were quite mixed. Although, as we have seen, it is to be expected with remakes that there will be some griping about the "pointlessness" of their existence, what is curious is the reframing and re-evaluation of the original 1989 adaptation within the reception of the more recent film. For example, Richard Lawson of *Variety* argued that, although campy, 'Lambert's film at least has a shabby grime to it, a drab ugliness that feels like the right kind of setting for King's miserable story [...] this new Pet Sematary is immediately too flashy, too bright for what's about to come' (Lawson, 2019). Meanwhile, others observed that while 'The original "Pet Sematary" may not be a critical darling [...] it is far superior to this inferior knockoff' (Rosza, 2019), or emphatically stated that they 'don't want to be buried with THIS Pet Sematary' (Lopez, 2019, emphasis in original). Within the majority of reviews it seemed, then, that *Pet Sematary* 1989 was undergoing a metamorphosis, being repositioned from a 'bland, cliched [and] cheap' (Harrington, 1989) adaptation to being closer to one of those 'culturally treasured' texts that Naremore speaks of.

Further think pieces began to emerge that appeared to place the 1989 film considerably above the 2019 version. The lasting effect of Mary Lambert's adaptation was highlighted, with *Slate* writer Jeffrey Bloomer noting he was 'forever scarred' by the film (Bloomer, 2019), while it was suggested that the key to the original's appeal was in its practical effects, which are 'generally much more pleasing than the iffy CGI effects found in the 2019 take' (Kennedy, 2019). Lambert's direction was underlined as a key positive aspect too, with it being argued that 'The enduring strength of Pet Sematary comes from the mood set by Lambert right from the start' (Cohen, 2019), and several writers noted that the release of the remake inspired them to revisit the original, which, as Tom Meisfjord wrote for Looper.com, 'still holds up decades after its debut' (Meisfjord, 2019). It would seem then that, as Linda Hutcheon argues, 'adaptation is not vampiric: it does not draw the life-blood from its source and leave it dying or dead [...] it may, on the contrary, keep that prior work alive, giving it an afterlife it would have never had otherwise' (2006: 175), with *Pet Sematary* 1989 being revisited and re-evaluted in the remake's wake.

As Forrest and Koos argue:

> almost all [remakes are] interesting for what they reveal, either about different cultures, about different directorial styles and aesthetic orientations, about class or gender perceptions, about different social-historical periods and changing audience expectations, about the dynamics of the genre film, or simply about the evolution of economic practices in the industry.
>
> (Forrest and Koos, 2001: 4–5)

These varied revelations can be discerned through identifying where remakes sever connective tissues to the original, of course, but can also be seen through examining where these connections remain intact. Given that the two films were released thirty years apart, directed by different people, and housed within different genre contexts, they are bound to be different at a narrative and aesthetic level, and these differences can tell us much. Firstly, however, I will explore some of the similarities the films share extratextually, and what these can tell us about their distinct places in the Stephen King cinematic corpus.

As illuminated in a previous chapter, efforts were made by both producer Richard P. Rubenstein and Mary Lambert to differentiate their film from its genre context, and shades of this insistence that *Pet Sematary* 1989 was "different" somehow can also be discerned in co-director Dennis Widmeyer's proclamation at *Pet Sematary* 2019's premiere that the film is 'not about vampires or werewolves. [Paramount] got behind it and say it is a very elevated horror film' (quoted in Hibberd, 2019). Widmeyer seemed to slightly recant on this statement in a later interview, where he noted that he did not mean "elevated" per say, but that the film is one that is 'not just concept-driven, that's actually trying to do a little more and it has some meat on the bone' (quoted in Vespe, 2019). Regardless of the term used, with both versions of *Pet Sematary* there was a seeming keenness to separate the respective films from the standard genre fare of their time. This similarity, however, begins to waver when we turn to the industrial and cultural context of the films.

Whereas the comments made by Rubenstein and Lambert at the time of the 1989 film's release were perhaps attempts to both separate *Pet Sematary* from the decade's horror output and reset the popular perception of Stephen King filmic adaptations at the time, the 2019 version is coming from a very different place, arriving in the midst of nostalgia horror's popularity, and a mere two years after what was termed 'The Year of Stephen King' in 2017 (Lambie, 2017). Following positive reviews of the miniseries adaptation of *11/23/63* (Hulu, 2016) and the cultural phenomenon that was the Stephen King influenced *Stranger Things* in 2016, 2017 saw the release of *It: Chapter One*, the success of which rekindled a thirst in all things King – as detailed above. This was reflected too in the positive reviews received by the Netflix adaptations of *Gerald's Game* (Mike Flanagan, 2017) and *1922* (Zak Hilditch, 2017), released in late September and October 2017 respectively. In addition to this, 2017 was not just the year of Stephen King, but a golden year for the horror genre more generally. *Get Out* (Jordan Peele, 2017), for instance, was nominated for four Academy Awards, winning the Oscar for Best Original Screenplay.[11] 2017 also saw the emergence of the contested term "post-horror", put forward by journalist Steve Rose to describe films such as *Hereditary*, *It Comes at Night* (Trey Edward Schults, 2017), and *A Ghost Story* (David Lowery, 2017), with the implication being that these films and others like them go beyond or are elevated above the 'restrictions' of the horror genre.[12] *Pet Sematary* 2019 – unlike its 1989 counterpart – makes no attempt to stand apart from its contemporary King adaptation brethren and, indeed, why would it, given its arrival at a time of renaissance for all things King? And, although it appears on the surface to be distancing itself from the broader horror genre, I would argue that Widmeyer's comments are an effort to actually adhere to a genre trend or label, with this trend being "post" or "elevated" horror. This can also be seen in the insistence of a studio publicist to journalist Jason Bailey that the film 'definitely fits the elevated genre' (Bailey, 2019).

These attempts to adhere, rather than stand apart, can also be discerned in the changes made to the narrative of *Pet Sematary* in the more recent adaptation. The addition of a pagan-esque processional of children wearing animal masks and beating a drum while taking a dog to the pet cemetery, for example, is not present in the 1989 film or the 1983 source material and is not brought up again after it occurs. However, this scene serves to emphasise a connection to the popular "folk gothic" subgenre, and films such as *The Witch* (Robert Eggers, 2015) and *Bloody Hell* (Alister Grierson, 2020). The scenes in which Louis and Rachel Creed (portrayed by Jason Clarke and Amy Seitmetz) discuss their differing opinions on life and death, present in the novel but barely there in the 1989 adaptation, also allow a mediation on the 'big metaphysical questions' that Steve Rose fears the standard offerings from the horror genre are 'too rigid' to engage with (Rose, 2017) and argues that post-horror is known for. Other changes made, such as Victor Pascow – whose role is greatly reduced – being portrayed by Obssa Ahmed, could have perhaps been utilised as an opportunity to address King's wider use of the problematic "Magical Negro" trope. In Kolsch and Widmeyer's film, however, this feels like an empty gesture and, if anything, supports this problematic trope rather than dismantling it.

Although *Pet Sematary* 2019 emerged amidst the burgeoning nostalgia horror trend, there is no real sense of nostalgia present within it for the 1989 version. There is something of a knowing wink in the scene where the Orinco truck barrels towards both Gage and Ellie shortly before Ellie's death – where the driver is distracted by a phone call from a 'Sheena' instead of singing along to "Sheena Is a Punk Rocker" by The Ramones – but overarchingly it seems that there was much more of a drive towards distancing the film from the previous cinematic version than anything else. Narrative changes result in the friendship between Louis and Jud (played here by John Lithgow) – one of the most developed relationships in the source novel and original 1989 film – being one of uneasy convenience rather than of genuine affection. And, although *Pet Sematary* 2019 does well to more fully flesh out the character of Rachel, the role of her parents and the tension between them and Louis is all but erased.

There is one last change that *Pet Sematary* 2019 makes that perhaps stands as its greatest act of severance from both the book and the 1989 adaptation, and it is one that I would be remiss to not discuss. One of the reasons why, as stated by producer Mark Vahradia, that it was decided that Ellie Creed would die in the remake, instead of Gage (this time played by Jete Lawrence and Hugo Lavoie/Lucas Lavoie respectively), was that 'we knew we had to have some surprises for people, otherwise they just go and watch the original' (quoted in Morgulis, 2019). As many have argued, in order for a remake to be considered on its own terms, it must both acknowledge the original film and depart from it. As Thomas Leitch notes, though, this is a commitment to a 'paradoxical promise: that they'll follow the original more closely than a sequel would, but that they'll differ more from the original, because they'll be better' (2001: 44). Perhaps this is the reason behind the creators of *Pet Sematary* 2019's initial insistence that their film was a straight readaptation of the 1983 source novel, rather than a remake of the 1989 version and why they debated the differences between these terms (Donato, 2019). Clearly, though, to ask an audience to disregard the earlier film entirely was virtually impossible and, after *Pet Sematary* 2019's release, there was a flurry of articles and think pieces comparing the two films, as has become de rigueur for coverage of remakes.

The main narrative change in *Pet Sematary* 2019 – the death of Ellie – was highlighted in several reviews as a sign that the 2019 film 'isn't afraid to go bleak' (Breznican,

2019a), and the ending in particular was presented as proof that this version had somehow dragged the story into even more cheerless territory (see for example Plante, 2019; Weiss, 2019). I venture, however, that the newer film never goes bleak enough. As argued in Chapter Two, a constant in the story of *Pet Sematary* is the sense of nihilism that pervades it. The 1989 adaptation is unrelenting in this respect, and even moves to make Louis Creed's fate less ambiguous than in the book: whereas the source novel ends with Rachel entering the kitchen and laying her hand on Louis's shoulder, the 1989 adaptation shows Rachel readying to stab Louis and we hear his scream. The 1989 film ends then with Church, Jud, Gage, and Louis dead; Rachel reanimated and Ellie in Chicago – the sole survivor of the Creed clan. The final scene of *Pet Sematary* 2019 meanwhile shows the reanimated Rachel, Ellie, Louis, and Church approach the car where the only living member of the family, Gage, sits. As the car chimes unlocked, we can safely assume that Gage will soon join his parents and sister in undeath. Although this ending seems darker at a surface level, the Creed family of 2019 end the film together, all be it as revenants (Figure 20). But this togetherness is a mercy not afforded to their 1983 or 1989 counterparts. Although sequels and remakes have different functions within the horror genre, and all three versions of the story discussed in this chapter were met with mixed reviews, the existence of *Pet Sematary 2*, and even more so the 2019 remake, speak to the longevity of *Pet Sematary*'s dark, unrelenting appeal.

Figure 20. Dead but together in Pet Sematary *2019*

Notes

1. *Pet Sematary* itself has been followed by the derivative *Pet Graveyard* (Rebecca Matthews, 2019).

2. With these being *Children of the Corn II: The Final Sacrifice* (David Price, 1992), *Children of the Corn III: Urban Harvest* (James D. R. Hickox, 1995), *Children of the Corn IV: The Gathering* (Greg Spence, 1996), *Children of the Corn V: Fields of Terror* (Ethan Wiley, 1998), and *Children of Corn 666: Isaac's Return* (Kari Skogland, 1999). Outside of the 1990s there has been several more sequels – *Children of the Corn: Revelation* (Guy Magar, 2001), *Children of the Corn: Genesis* (Joel Soisson, 2011), and *Children of the Corn: Runaway* (John Gulager, 2018). There has also been a television remake of the original film directed by Donald P. Borchers and released in 2009, and a prequel film, also entitled *Children of the Corn*.

3. A keen-eyed viewer will no doubt notice that this is not the same house from the original film, with the production of the sequel taking place in Georgia rather than Maine.

4. Other bands included on the soundtrack are The Jesus and Mary Chain, and Miranda Sex Garden. The majority of bands on the *Pet Sematary 2* soundtrack are either female fronted and/or made up entirely of women. Both Traci Lords and Jan King recorded songs specifically for the soundtrack, "Love Never Dies" and "Fading Away" respectively. The Ramones also return in the form of "Poison Heart" in the film's credits.

5. Another text with an array of Stephen King references is *Fear Street: 1978* (Leigh Janiak, 2021) – in which a character is said to 'like Stephen King and spiders' and responds 'First of all, Stephen King is like, super popular' – he later (sarcastically) suggests setting up a Stephen King reading club.

6. Not least the presence of Finn Wolfhard as Richie Tozier, who plays Mike Wheeler in *Stranger Things*.

7. At least until the second season, where she is joined by Max.

8. See Cunningham (2012) and D'Alessandro (2019). It should be noted that *The Breathing Method* adaptation at least – given the date of Cunningham's report – was not set in motion as a result of the success of *IT*.

9. Remakes of *The Tommyknockers* and *The Dark Half* (George A. Romero, 1993) have been reported to be in production too (see Kit, 2018 and Fleming Jr., 2019).

10. For a detailed and considered account of North American remakes 2003–2013, see Mee (2022).

11. *Get Out*'s writer/director Jordan Peele was the first black person to win this award.

12. For an excellent discussion and analysis of this concept, see Church (2020).

Legacy and conclusion: 'Here's to your bones'

This book opened by describing the presence of a pet cemetery in "Dial Z for Zombie", a segment of *The Simpsons* episode "Treehouse of Horror III". In the same year, a poster for *Pet Sematary* appeared in *Wayne's World* (Penelope Spheeris, 1992) in the bedroom of Cassandra. These early nods to the film have been joined since by mentions and references in a vast array of media, in sources as varied as cartoon *The Spooktacular New Adventures of Casper* (Fox Kids, 1996–1998), sitcom *Everybody Loves Raymond* (CBS, 1996–2005), and anarchic animation *South Park* (Comedy Central, 1997–). Perhaps the most incongruous reference can be found in superhero blockbuster *Justice League* (Zack Snyder, 2017) when The Flash asks if resurrecting Superman from the dead will result in a 'Pet Sematary scenario'. In terms of *Pet Sematary*'s legacy within the horror genre specifically, direct references can be found in *Pumpkinhead II: Blood Wings* (Jeff Burr, 1994) and meta-horror *Behind the Mask: The Rise of Leslie Vernon* (Scott Glosserman, 2006), where the titular character has two pet turtles named Church and Zowie. Outside of horror cinema, long-running television series *Supernatural* (The WB, 2005–2006/The CW, 2006–2020) has referenced *Pet Sematary*, and in the music video for Frnkiero and the Cellabration's "Weighted", the lead singer is brought back to life by a group of young fans who abscond from the funeral home with his body and bury it in the 'Pet Sematary' marked on their map. In subsequent Stephen King adaptations too –– the 1997 miniseries *The Shining*, *Mr. Mercedes* (Audience, 2017–2019) and the King-inspired *Castle Rock* – intertextual nods to *Pet Sematary* are also included.

Within this volume, I have addressed several crucial gaps in horror scholarship, and have sought to retrieve *Pet Sematary* from considerations of how the narrative functions within the Gothic tradition. I have presented it instead as part of the "grief horror" genre, reframing its central themes firmly within its 1980s production context. The decade in which *Pet Sematary* emerged saw the horror genre gaining a rapid level of visibility, during which the cultural capital of Stephen King as a cinematic brand rose, peaked, and fell. It is not hyperbolic to claim that Lambert's film, arriving right at the end of the 1980s, and simultaneously adhering to and departing from 1980s genre tropes, played a significant role in changing the popular perception of King films and their commercial viability. Despite this, *Pet Sematary* thus far has been neglected in favour of those adaptations that were more "serious" genre fare, or those that were helmed by directors considered to be "auteurs". Of course, *Pet Sematary* is not the only King adaptation to suffer this lack of critical engagement, and this book joins the growing number of accounts that seek to revisit and revise our understanding and appreciation of previous King adaptations, particularly in light of the recent renaissance of interest in his works within popular culture. While many films throughout horror history have been rightly recognised as engaging with the cultural anxieties of their production period – particularly the 1970s realist horror films that I drew comparisons to earlier – *Pet Sematary*'s ability to do this has been understudied, despite the fact that its themes resonate strongly with the film's wider cultural context. Within the previous chapters, for instance, I have highlighted the centrality of the family and the American Dream – both recurrent King conventions – to 1980s political rhetoric in particular, and identified how these concepts are sketched in *Pet Sematary* only to be torn asunder. The problematic presence of the "Indian Burial Ground" too speaks to the specific period of time in Maine within which the film and novel were created.

The ongoing broader cultural relevance and recognition of *Pet Sematary* has been underlined by the release of *Unearthed and Untold: The Path to Pet Sematary*, a documentary focusing on the production of the film and memories of various cast and crew, as well as retrospectives such as UCLA's Film and Television Archive presenting the event 'Spirits in the Sky: A Weekend with Mary Lambert' at the Billy Wilder Theater in August 2019. *Pet Sematary* may not yet have been canonised as a 'classic' horror film in the same way as its adaptation cousins, *The Shining* and *Carrie*, but, as this volume has shown, there is clearly an argument for its placement as a culturally treasured horror film. I only hope that in the preceding pages I have managed to give the film the proper consideration it deserves.

The ongoing references to *Pet Sematary* detailed above, some decades after its release, speak to the longevity of its impact on the horror genre and popular culture, and we will soon return to the story with a prequel film, which is to be part of Paramount's new streaming service Paramount+.[1] Perhaps it is the archetypal quality of the story and its characters that entice us to revisit *Pet Sematary*, or perhaps it is its painful and raw depiction of the process of grief. Whatever the reason, this continuation of the *Pet*

Sematary story, almost forty years after its publication, and more than thirty years after Lambert's film, shows that we will, much like the good doctor Creed, be tempted to climb the deadfall again and again.

Figure 21. One last caress

Notes

1. Interestingly, this new *Pet Sematary* story will be directed by another woman, Lindsey Beer (Squires, 2021).

Bibliography

Adams, T. (2000) 'Constant Craving', *The Guardian*. 17 September. Available at: https://www.theguardian.com/books/2000/sep/17/stephenking.fiction1 (Accessed: 30/03/2022).

Alegre, S. M. (2001) 'Nightmares of Childhood: The Child and the Monster in Four Novels by Stephen King', *Atlantis*, 23(3), pp. 105–114.

Andreeva, N. (2021) '"The Shining" Offshoot Series "Overlook" From Bad Robot Not Going Forward At HBO Max, Closing In On New Home', *Deadline*. 4 August. Available at: https://deadline.com/2021/08/the-shining-overlook-bad-robot-dead-hbo-max-new-home-jj-abrams-stephen-king-1234808746/ (Accessed: 23/11/2022).

Anon. (1999) 'The Terror Teletype', *Fangoria*, 179, p. 9.

Ansen, D. (1982) 'Frozen Slime', *Newsweek*, June 28, p. 73.

Armstrong, J. (2016) 'Gothic Matters of De-Composition: The Pastoral Dead in Contemporary American Fiction', *Text Matters: A Journal of Literature, Theory and Culture*, 6(6), pp. 127–143.

Badley, L. (2009) 'Bringing It All Back Home: Horror Cinema and Video Culture', in Conrich, I. (ed.) *Horrorzone: The Cultural Experience of Contemporary Horror Cinema*. London: IB Tauris, pp. 45–63.

Bailey, J. (2019) '"Pet Sematary" and the Sticky Wicket of "Elevated Horror"', *Flavorwire*. 4 April. Available at: https://www.flavorwire.com/616170/pet-sematary-and-the-sticky-wicket-of-elevated-horror (Accessed: 02/07/2021).

Balanzalegui, J. (2018) *The Uncanny Child in Transnational Cinema: Ghosts of Futurity at the Turn of the Twenty-First Century*. Amsterdam: Amsterdam University Press.

Bangs, L. (1988) *Psychotic Reactions and Carburetor Dung*. New York: Vintage Books.

Barnum, C. (2010) 'A Single Penny, an Inch of Land, or an Ounce of Sovereignty: The Problem of Tribal Sovereignty and Water Quality Regulation under the Maine Indian Claims Settlement Act', *Ecology Law Quarterly*, 37(4), pp. 1159–1216.

BBC (2021) 'Canada: 751 Unmarked Graves Found at Residential School', *BBC*. 24 June. Available at: https://www.bbc.co.uk/news/world-us-canada-57592243 (Accessed: 15/07/2021).

Bell, J. (2013) *Gothic: The Dark Heart of Film*. London: British Film Institute.

Benshoff, H. M. (2014) 'Preface', in Benshoff, H. M. (ed.) *A Companion to the Horror Film*. New Jersey: John Wiley & Sons, pp. xiii–xix.

Bergland, R. L. (2000) *The National Uncanny: Indian Ghosts and American Subjects*. Hanover: Dartmouth College Press.

Beschloss, M. (2016) 'The Ad That Helped Reagan Sell Good Times to an Uncertain Nation', *New York Times*. 7 May. Available at: https://www.nytimes.com/2016/05/08/business/the-ad-that-helped-reagan-sell-good-times-to-an-uncertain-nation.html (Accessed: 04/08/2021).

Bettinson, G. (2015) 'Resurrecting Carrie', in Clayton, W. (ed.) *Style and Form in the Hollywood Slasher Film*. New York: Palgrave MacMillan, pp. 131–145.

Blake, L. (2008) *The Wounds of Nations: Horror Cinema, Historical Trauma and National Identity*. Manchester: Manchester University Press.

Bloom, H. (2003) 'For the World of Letters, It's a Horror', *Los Angeles Times*. 19 September. Available at: https://www.latimes.com/archives/la-xpm-2003-sep-19-oe-bloom19-story.html (Accessed: 09/07/2021).

Bloomer, J. (2019) '*Pet Sematary* Cursed a Generation (With an Inability to Spell Cemetery)', *Slate*. 4 April. Available at: https://slate.com/culture/2019/04/pet-sematary-spelling-stephen-king-book-movie-cemetery.html (Accessed: 03/07/2021).

Boyd, C. E. (2009) '"You See Your Culture Coming Out of the Ground Like a Power": Uncanny Narratives in Time and Space on the Northwest Coast', *Ethnohistory*, 56(2), pp. 699–731.

Brewster, F., Fenton, H., and Morris, M. (2005) *Shock! Horror!: Astounding Artwork from the Video Nasty Era*. Surrey: FAB Press.

Breznican, A. (2019a) 'Pet Sematary Exhumed: Stephen King Looks Back At His Most Disturbing Story', *Entertainment Weekly*. 29 March. Available at: https://ew.com/movies/2019/03/29/pet-sematary-stephen-king-interview/ (Accessed: 03/07/2021).

Breznican, A. (2019b) 'Original Pet Sematary Director Unearths Secrets Of The 1989 Horror Classic', *Entertainment Weekly*. 4 April. Available at: https://ew.com/movies/2019/04/04/pet-sematary-1989-mary-lambert-director/ (Accessed: 03/07/2021).

Brodeur, P. (1985) *Restitution: The Land Claims of the Mashpee, Passamaquoddy, and Penobscot Indians of New England*. Boston: Northeastern University Press.

Brophy, P. (1986) 'Horrality – The Textual of Contemporary Horror Films', reprinted in Gelder, K. (ed.) (2000) *The Horror Reader*. New York: Routledge, pp. 276–284.

Brown, B. (2009) 'The Lighter Side of Grief: Loss in Contemporary American Cinema', *Visual Anthropology*, 22(1), pp. 30–43.

Brown, S. (2018) *Screening Stephen King: Adaptations and the Horror Genre in Film and Television*. Austin: University of Texas Press.

Brown, S. (2019) *Creepshow (Devil's Advocates)*. Leighton Buzzard: Auteur.

Browning, M. (2009) *Stephen King Films on the Big Screen*. Bristol: Intellect.

Burger, A. (2016) *Teaching Stephen King: Horror, The Supernatural, and New Approaches to Literature*. New York: Palgrave McMillan.

Campopiano, J. and White, J. (2017) *Unearthed and Untold: The Path to Pet Sematary*. USA: Ocean's Light Productions.

Canby, V. (1982) '"The Thing", Horror and Science Fiction', *The New York Times*. 25 June. Available at: https://www.nytimes.com/1982/06/25/movies/the-thing-horror-and-science-fiction.html (Accessed: 08/08/2021).

Carroll, P. N. (1990) *It Seemed Like Nothing Happened: America in the 1970s*. New Brunswick: Rutgers University Press.

Castricano, C. J. (2001) *Cryptomimesis: The Gothic and Jacque Derrida's Ghost Writing*. Montreal: McGill-Queen's University Press.

Caterine, D. V. (2014) 'Heirs through Fear: Indian Curses, Accursed Indian Lands, and White Christian Sovereignty in America', *Nova Religio: The Journal of Alternative and Emergent Religions*, 18(1), pp. 37–57.

Century, S. (2018) 'Horror Sequels and the Female Director', *Syfy*. 27 July. https://www.syfy.com/syfywire/horror-sequels-and-the-female-director (Accessed: 03/07/2021; no longer available).

Chippindale, P. (1982) 'How High Street Horror is Invading the Home', *The Sunday Times*, 23 May.

Church, D. (2020) *Post Horror: Art, Genre and Cultural Elevation.* Edinburgh: Edinburgh University Press.

Clover, C. (1987) 'Her Body, Himself: Gender in the Slasher Film', reprinted in Grant, B. K. (ed.) (2015) *The Dread of Difference: Gender and The Horror Film*. Austin: University of Texas Press, pp. 68–115.

Clover, C. (1992) *Men, Women and Chainsaws: Gender in the Modern Horror Film.* Updated Edition (2015). Princeton: Princeton University Press.

Coffel, C. (2018) '"Unearthed & Untold" Directors Talk About the Path to "Pet Sematary [Interview]', *Bloody Disgusting*. 19 March. Available at: https://bloody-disgusting.com/interviews/3488754/interview/ (Accessed: 25/06/2021).

Cohen, A. (2019) 'The Underrated Original Pet Sematary Proves That "Sometimes, Dead Is Better"', *Refinery29*. 9 April. Available at: https://www.refinery29.com/en-gb/2019/04/229309/pet-sematary-1989-review-director-mary-lambert (Accessed: 03/07/2021).

Collings, M. (1987) *The Stephen King Phenomenon*. Mercer Island, WA: Starmont House.

Collis, C. (2017) 'Magazine of the Living Dead: The Bloody Rise And Frightful Fall Of Fangoria' *Entertainment Weekly*. 11 October. Available at: https://ew.com/movies/2017/10/11/fangoria/ (Accessed: 25/06/2021).

Cook, P. (2012) 'No Fixed Address: The Women's Picture from Outrage to Blue Steel', in Gledhill, C. (ed.) *Gender Meets Genre in Postwar Cinemas*. Champaign: University of Illinois Press, pp. 54–67.

Craig, P. and Fradley, M. (2010) 'Teenage Traumata: Youth, Affective Politics, and the Contemporary American Horror Film', in Hantke, S. (ed.) *American Horror Film: The Genre at the Turn of the Millennium*. Jackson: University Press of Mississippi, pp. 77–102.

Crampton, B. (2016) 'Barbara Crampton: Don't Call Me A Scream Queen', *Birth Movies Death.* 15 December. Available at: https://birthmoviesdeath.com/2016/12/15/barbara-crampton-dont-call-me-a-scream-queen (Accessed: 03/07/2021).

Cunningham, J. (2012) '"Sinister" Director Scott Derrickson Will Learn Stephen King's "Breathing Method"', *Indie Wire.* 16 October. Available at: https://www.indiewire.com/2012/10/sinister-director-scott-derrickson-will-learn-stephen-kings-breathing-method-250765/ (Accessed: 30/03/2022).

D'Alessandro, A. (2019) 'Andre Ovredal To Direct Stephen King's "The Long Walk" For New Line', *Deadline.* 21 May. Available at: https://deadline.com/2019/05/stephen-king-the-long-walk-new-line-movie-andre-ovredal-directing-1202620157/ (Accessed: 23/11/22).

Davis, C. S. and Crane, J. L. (2015) 'A Dialogue with (Un)Death: Horror Films as a Discursive Attempt to Construct a Relationship with the Dead', *Journal of Loss and Trauma*, 20(5), pp. 417–429.

Dickey, C. (2016) 'The Suburban Horror of the Indian Burial Ground', *New Republic.* 19 October. Available at: https://newrepublic.com/article/137856/suburban-horror-indian-burial-ground (Accessed: 04/08/2021).

Dickinson, J. (2015) 'The Void Interview With Steven Kostanski', *Scream.* 26 March. Available at: https://www.screamhorrormag.com/the-void-interview-with-steven-sostanski/ (Accessed: 25/06/2021).

Donato, M. (2019) '"Pet Sematary" Directors Talk "Friday the 13th," The Ramones & Getting Stephen King Right', *Atom Tickets*. 8 April. Available at: https://atomtickets.com/movie-news/pet-sematary-interview-dennis-widmyer-kevin-kolsch/ (Accessed: 08/08/2021).

Donnelly, K. (2018) *The Shining (Cultographies)*. London: Wallflower Press.

Dymond, E. J. (2013) 'From the Present to the Past: An Exploration of Family Dynamics in Stephen King's Pet Sematary', *Journal of Popular Culture*, 46(4), pp. 789–810.

Easton, N. J. (1989) '"Pet Sematary" Buries the Competition', *Los Angeles Times*. 25 April. Available at: https://www.latimes.com/archives/la-xpm-1989-04-25-ca-1554-story.html (Accessed: 03/07/2021).

Edwards-Behi, N. (2017) 'Cinema: A Response to Post-Horror', *Wales Arts Review*. 9 June. Available at: https://www.walesartsreview.org/cinema-a-response-to-post-horror/ (Accessed: 31/07/2021).

Elliott, K. (2007) *Rethinking the Novel/Film Debate*. Cambridge: Cambridge University Press.

Evangelista, C. (2019) '1989 "Pet Sematary" Director Mary Lambert On Working With Stephen King, Going Dark, "Pet Sematary 2" and More [Interview]', *Slashfilm*. 1 April. Available at: https://www.slashfilm.com/mary-lambert-interview/ (Accessed: 03/07/2021).

Fahy, T. (2019) 'The Duffer Brothers' Stranger Things (2016 – Present): Horror and Nostalgia', in Bacon, S. (ed.) *Horror: A Companion*. Oxford: Pet Lang Ltd, pp. 103–109.

Ferrante, A. C. (1995) 'News', *Fangoria*, 148, p. 8.

Fienberg, D. (2016) 'The Duffer Brothers Talk "Stranger Things" Influences, "It" Dreams and Netflix Phase 2', *Hollywood Reporter*. 1 August. Available at: https://www.hollywoodreporter.com/tv/tv-news/duffer-brothers-talk-stranger-things-916180/ (Accessed: 03/07/2021).

Fleming Jr., M. (2019) '"Her Smell" Helmer Alex Ross Perry To Adapt & Direct Stephen King Novel "The Dark Half" For MGM', *Deadline*. 11 December. Available at: https://deadline.com/2019/12/stephen-king-alex-ross-perry-stephen-king-novel-the-dark-half-mgm-her-smell-1202801641/ (Accessed: 30/03/2022).

Forrest, J. and Koos, L. R. (2001) 'Reviewing Remakes: An Introduction', in Forrest, J. and Koos, L. R. (eds.) *Dead Ringers: The Remake in Theory and Practice*. Albany: State University of New York Press, pp. 1–36.

Freeland, C. (1996) 'Feminist Frameworks for Horror Films', in Bordwell, D. and Carroll, N. (eds.) *Post Theory: Reconstructing Film Studies*. Madison: University of Wisconsin Press, pp. 195–218.

Freeman, H. (2017) 'From Black Mirror to Stranger Things, Why Do We Keep Going Back To The 80s?', *The Guardian*. 18 February. Available at: https://www.theguardian.com/tv-and-radio/2017/feb/18/stranger-things-why-tv-is-obsessed-with-the-80s (Accessed: 06/08/2021).

Freidman, L. D. and Kavey, A. B. (2016) *Monstrous Progeny: A History of the Frankenstein Narratives*. New Brunswick: Rutgers University Press.

Galuppo, M. (2017) 'Director Karyn Kusama on Sundance Horror Movie: "Women Have a Lot to Be Really F-ing Afraid Of"', *Hollywood Reporter*. 12 January. Available at: https://www.hollywoodreporter.com/movies/movie-features/director-karyn-kusama-sundance-horror-movie-women-have-a-lot-be-f-ing-afraid-965251/ (Accessed: 03/07/2021).

Gill, P. (2002) 'The Monstrous Years: Teens, Slasher Films, and the Family', *Journal of Film and Video*, 54(4), pp. 16–30.

Godfrey, A. (2017) 'Raw Director Julia Ducournau: "Cannibalism is part of humanity"', *The Guardian*. 30 March. Available at: https://www.theguardian.com/film/2017/mar/30/raw-director-julia-ducournau-cannibalism-is-part-of-humanity (Accessed: 04/08/2021).

Goldstein, P. (1986) 'Movie Review: "Maximum Overdrive" Spins Its Wheels', *Los Angeles Times*. 28 July. Available at: https://www.latimes.com/archives/la-xpm-1986-07-28-ca-18553-story.html (Accessed: 07/09/2020).

Grant, B. K. (1992) 'Taking Back the Night of the Living Dead: George Romero, Feminism, and the Horror Film', reprinted in Grant, B. K. (ed.) (2015) *The Dread of Difference: Gender and The Horror Film*. Austin: University of Texas Press, pp. 228–240.

Greene, A. (2014) 'Stephen King: The Rolling Stone Interview', *Rolling Stone*. 31 October. Available at: http://www.rollingstone.com/culture/features/stephen-king-the-rolling-stone-interview-20141031?page=5 (Accessed: 03/07/2021).

Gross, E. (1986) 'Stephen King Takes a Vacation', *Fangoria*, 58, pp. 22–25.

Handler, R. (2021) 'Titane Director Julia Ducournau Doesn't See Herself As a Film Festival Provocateur', *Vulture*. 16 July. Available at: https://www.vulture.com/2021/07/titanes-julia-ducournau-doesnt-think-shes-a-provocateur.html (Accessed: 08/08/2021).

Hantke, S. (2010) 'Introduction – They Don't Make 'Em Like They Used To: On the Rhetoric of Crisis and the Current State of American Horror Cinema', in Hantke, S. (ed.) *American Horror Film: The Genre at the Turn of the Millennium*. Jackson: University Press of Mississippi, pp. 7–29.

Harber, S. (2019) 'Why Pet Sematary 2 Is an Underrated Stephen King Movie', *Den of Geek*. 28 August. Available at: https://www.denofgeek.com/movies/pet-sematary-2-underrated-stephen-king-movie/ (Accessed: 03/08/2021).

Harmetz, A. (1984) '"Pet" Film Rights Sold', *New York Times*. 8 June. Available at: https://www.nytimes.com/1984/06/08/movies/pet-film-rights-sold.html (Accessed: 03/07/2021).

Harrington, R. (1989) 'Pet Sematary', *Washington Post*. 22 April. Available at: https://www.washingtonpost.com/wp-srv/style/longterm/movies/videos/petsemataryrharrington_a0aab5.htm??noredirect=on (Accessed: 03/07/2021).

Harrison, E. (2021) '"Madonna told me she wanted to f*** a Black guy on the altar" claims Like a Prayer director', *The Independent*. 9 April. Available at: https://www.independent.co.uk/arts-entertainment/music/news/madonna-like-a-prayer-music-video-b1828947.html (Accessed: 04/08/2021).

Hebdige, D. (1983) 'Rape of Our Children's Minds', *Daily Mail*, 30 June. P. 6.

Heller Nicholas, A. (2018) 'Ladykillers: An A–Z of Women's Horror Filmmaking', *Vulture*. 5 December. Available at: https://www.vulture.com/2018/12/womens-horror-films-beginners-guide.html (Accessed: 03/07/2021).

Herron, D. (1988) 'The Summation', in Herron, D. (ed.) *Reign of Fear: The Fiction and Film of Stephen King (1982–1989)*. London: Pan Books, pp. 209–247.

Hibberd, J. (2019) '*Pet Sematary* Remake: First Reactions from SXSW', *Entertainment Weekly*. 17 March. Available at: https://ew.com/movies/2019/03/17/pet-sematary-first-reactions-sxsw/ (Accessed: 03/07/2021).

Hicks, D. (1980) 'Too Far – Postal Zone', *Fangoria*, 9, p. 5.

Holt, J. (2007) '1989. Movies and the American Dream', in Prince, S. (ed.) *American Cinema of the 1980s: Themes and Variations*. New Brunswick: Rutgers University Press, pp. 210–232.

Hopkins, L. (2005) *Screening the Gothic*. Austin: University of Texas Press.

Hoppenstand, G. and Browne, R. B. (1987) 'The Horror of It All: Stephen King and the Landscape of the American Nightmare', in Hoppenstand, G. and Browne, R. B. (eds.) *The Gothic World of Stephen King: Landscape of Nightmares*. Bowling Green: Bowling Green State University Press, pp. 1–19.

Hughes, D. (1990) 'Dead Pets Society', *Starburst*, 137, pp. 11–13.

Hunter, A. (1987) 'The Role of Liberal Political Culture in the Construction of Middle America', *University of Miami Law Review*, 42(1), pp. 93–126.

Hutcheon, L. (2006) *A Theory of Adaptation*. New York: Routledge.

Hutchings, P. (1993) 'Masculinity and the Horror Film', in Kirkham, P. and Thumim, J. (eds.) *You Tarzan: Masculinity, Movies and Men*. London: Lawrence & Wishart, pp. 77–90.

Hutchings, P. (1996) 'Tearing Your Soul Apart: Horror's New Monsters', in Sage, V. and Smith, A. L. (eds.) *Modern Gothic: A Reader*. Manchester: Manchester University Press.

Hutchings, P. (2004) *The Horror Film*. Edinburgh: Pearson Longman.

Jancovich, M. (2001) 'Genre and the Audience: Genre Classifications and Cultural Distinctions in the Mediation of *The Silence of the Lambs*', in Stokes, M. and Maltby, R. (eds.) *Hollywood Spectatorship Changing Perceptions of Cinema Audiences*. London: BFI Publishing, pp. 33–45.

Janicker, R. (2007) 'The Horrors of Maine: Space, Place and Regionalism in Stephen King's Pet Sematary', *U.S. Studies Online: The BAAS Postgraduate Journal*, 11. Available at: https://baas.ac.uk/baas-archive/issue-11-autumn-2007-article-2/ (Accessed: 08/08/2021).

Jess-Cooke, C. (2009) *Film Sequels: Theory and Practice from Hollywood to Bollywood*. Edinburgh: Edinburgh University Press.

Jess-Cooke, C. and Verevis, C. (2010) *Second Takes: Approaches to the Film Sequel*. Albany: State University of New York Press.

Jones, S. (2013) *Torture Porn: Popular Horror After Saw*. New York: Palgrave MacMillan.

Jones, S. (2021) 'The Metamodern Slasher Film', presented at: Kurja Polt Genre Film Festival. Ljubljana: Slovenia.

Keesey, D. (2015) *Brian De Palma's Split-Screen: A Life in Film*. Jackson: University Press of Mississippi.

Keesey, D. (2018) 'Psychoanalysis of a Sequel: The Disinterment of Pet Sematary Two', *Irish Journal of Gothic and Horror Studies*, 7, pp. 23–33.

Kehr, D. (1989) '"Pet Sematary" Buries Magic Found in Stephen King', *Chicago Tribune*. 24 April. Available at: https://www.chicagotribune.com/news/ct-xpm-1989-04-24-8904060819-story.html (Accessed: 03/07/2021).

Kempers, M. (1989) 'There's Losing and Winning: Ironies of the Maine Indian Land Claim', *Legal Studies Forum*, 13(3), pp. 267–299.

Kendrick, J. (2014) 'Slasher Films and Gore in the 1980s', in Benshoff, H. M. (ed.) *A Companion to the Horror Film*. West Sussex: Wiley-Blackwell, pp. 310–328.

Kennedy, M. (2019) 'Which Pet Sematary Movie Is Better? 1989 vs. 2019', *Screenrant*. 24 May. Available at: https://screenrant.com/pet-sematary-movies-1989-2019-comparison-better/ (Accessed: 03/07/2021).

King, S. (1983) *Pet Sematary*. New York: Double Day.

King, S. [@StephenKing] (2016) [Twitter] 17 July. Available at: https://twitter.com/stephenking/status/754699429047836672 (Accessed: 08/08/2021).

King, S. [@StephenKing] (2017) [Twitter] 16 July. Available at: https://twitter.com/StephenKing/status/886710019756085248 (Accessed: 31/07/2021).

Kit, B. (2018) 'Universal Wins Stephen King's "Tommyknockers" Bidding War', *Hollywood Reporter*. 20 April. Available at: https://www.hollywoodreporter.com/movies/movie-news/univeral-wins-stephen-kings-tommyknockers-bidding-war-1104737/ (Accessed: 30/03/2022).

Kit, B. (2020) 'Lynne Ramsey to Direct Stephen King Adaptation "The Girl Who Loved Tom Gordon"', *Hollywood Reporter*. 16 November. Available at: https://www.hollywoodreporter.com/movies/movie-news/lynne-ramsay-to-direct-stephen-king-adaptation-the-girl-who-loved-tom-gordon-4092922/ (Accessed: 30/03/2022).

Kogan, R. (1986) 'King's a Horror at Directing', *Chicago Tribune*, 29 July, p. 3.

Kooyman, B. (2010) 'How the Masters of Horror Master Their Personae: Self-Fashioning at Play in the Masters of Horror DVD Extras', in Hantke, S. (ed.) *American Horror Film: The Genre at the Turn of the Millennium*. Jackson: University Press of Mississippi, pp. 193–220.

Kord, T. S. (2016) *Little Horrors: How Cinema's Evil Children Play on Our Guilt*. Jefferson: McFarland and Co.

Kvaran, K. M. (2016) '"You're All Doomed!" A Socioeconomic Analysis of Slasher Films', *Journal of American Studies*, 50(4), pp. 953–970.

Labbe, R. A. (1988) 'Paying Respects at Pet Sematary', *Fangoria*, 8, pp. 18–21.

Labbe, R. A. (1990) 'Ratman', *Fangoria*, 99, pp. 32–34, 59.

Labbe, R. A. (2014) 'Pet Sematary Memories: Part Two', *Fangoria*, 330, pp. 18–19, 80–81.

Lambert, M. (2019) 'Director's Commentary', *Pet Sematary 30th Anniversary Blu-ray*. USA: Paramount Home Entertainment.

Lambie, R. (2017) 'Why 2017 Was the Year of Stephen King on Screen', *DenofGeek*. December 8. Available at: https://www.denofgeek.com/culture/why-2017-was-the-year-of-stephen-king-on-screen/ (Accessed: 23/11/2022).

Landis, J. (1980) 'A Solicited Letter – Postal Zone', *Fangoria*, 9, p. 5.

Lanzagorta, M. (2006) 'The Gruesome Gazettes Part 2: Fangoria and Beyond', *Popmatters*. 16 August. Available at: https://www.popmatters.com/lanzagorta060817-2496179115.html (Accessed: 25/06/2021).

Lawson, R. (2019) '*Pet Sematary* Should Have Stayed Dead', *Vanity Fair*. 4 April. Available at: https://www.vanityfair.com/hollywood/2019/04/pet-sematary-review (Accessed on: 03/07/2021).

Lehman-Haupt, C. (1986) 'It', *New York Times*. 21 August. Available at: https://www.nytimes.com/1986/08/21/books/it.html (Accessed: 03/07/2021).

Leitch, T. (2001) 'Twice-Told Tales: Disavowal and the Rhetoric of the Remake', in Forrest, J. and Koos, L. R. (eds.) *Dead Ringers: The Remake in Theory and Practice*. Albany: State University of New York Press, pp. 37–62.

Leppert, A. (2019) *TV Family Values: Gender, Domestic Labor, and 1980s Sitcoms*. New Brunswick: Rutgers University Press.

Lodge, G. (2018) 'The horror of grief: how loss is the ultimate boogeyman in Hereditary', *The Guardian*. 7 June. Available at: https://www.theguardian.com/film/2018/jun/07/hereditary-toni-collette-horror-grief (Accessed: 02/07/2021).

Lopez, K. (2019) 'Pet Sematary is a film best life dead and buried', *Culturess*. 4 April. Available at: https://culturess.com/2019/04/04/pet-sematary-review-film-best-left-dead-and-buried/ (Accessed: 04/08/2021).

Lowenstein, A. (2005) *Shocking Representations: Historical Trauma, National Cinema and the Modern Horror Film*. New York: Columbia University Press.

Lowenstein, A. (2015) 'Feminine Horror: The Embodied Surrealism of *In My Skin*', in Grant, B. K. (ed.) *The Dread of Difference: Gender and the Horror Film*. Austin: University of Texas Press, pp. 470–487.

Luckhurst, R. (2013) *The Shining*. London: BFI.

Luers, E. (2016) 'Mary Lambert on Pet Sematary, Non-Linear Narratives and Child Actors', *Filmmaker Magazine*. 15 June. Available at: https://filmmakermagazine.com/98862-mary-lambert-pet-sematary-non-linear-narratives-and-child-actors/#.YKqBjKhKjlX (Accessed: 03/07/2021).

MacKenthun, G. (1998) 'Haunted Real Estate: The Occlusion of Colonial Dispossession and Signatures of Cultural Survival in U.S. Horror Fiction', *Amerikastudien/American Studies*, 43(1), pp. 93–108.

Magistrale, T. (1988) 'Hawthorne's Woods Revisited: Stephen King's "Pet Sematary"' *Nathanial Hawthorne Review*, 14(1), pp. 9–13.

Magistrale, T. (2003) *Hollywood's Stephen King*. New York: Palgrave Macmillan.

Malcolm, D. (1980) 'Stanley Kubrick's The Shining – Review', *The Guardian*. 2 October. Available at: https://www.theguardian.com/film/2014/oct/02/the-shining-stanley-kubrick-jack-nicholson-review-1980 (Accessed: 04/08/2021).

Malmquist, A. (1979) 'More Fantasy – Postal Zone', *Fangoria*, 2, p. 6.

Marcus, D. (2004) *Happy Days and Wonder Years: The Fifties and the Sixties in Contemporary Cultural Politics*. New Brunswick: Rutgers University Press.

Marks, L. (2012) 'The Horror, the Horror: Women Gather in LA for Viscera Film Festival', *The Guardian*. 12 July. Available at: https://www.theguardian.com/film/2012/jul/12/viscera-festival-los-angeles (Accessed: 03/07/2021).

Martin, B. (1981) 'Imagination Inc.', *Fangoria*, 10, p. 4.

Martin, D. (2015) *Extreme Asia: The Rise of Cult Cinema from the Far East*. Edinburgh: Edinburgh University Press.

Martin, R. K. and Savoy, E. (1998) 'Introduction', in Martin, R. K. and Savoy, E. (eds.) *American Gothic: New Interventions in a National Narrative*. Iowa City: University of Iowa Press, pp. viii–xii.

Maslin, J. (1982) 'Film View: Bloodbaths Debase Movies and Audience', *New York Times*. 21 November. Available at: https://www.nytimes.com/1982/11/21/movies/film-view-bloodbaths-debase-movies-and-audiences.html (Accessed: 03/07/2021).

Mathijs, E. (2009) 'They're Here!: Special Effects in Horror Cinema of the 1970s and 1980s', in Conrich, I. (ed.) *Horrorzone: The Cultural Experience of Contemporary Horror Cinema*. London: IB Tauris, pp. 153–171.

Matthews, T. (2005) 'The End of Innocence: Stand by Me 19 Years Late', *Creative Screenwriting*, 12(5), pp. 69–73.

McAleer, P. (2011) 'I Have the Whole World in My Hands… Now What?: Power, Control, Responsibility and the Baby Boomers in Stephen King's Fiction', *The Journal of Popular Culture*, 44(6), pp. 1209–1227.

McCarthy, K. (2019) 'Remember Things: Consumerism, Nostalgia, and Geek Culture in Stranger Things', *Journal of Popular Culture*, 52(3), pp. 663–677.

McLaughlin, T. (1981) 'Tasty Reading – Postal Zone', *Fangoria*, 10, p. 5.

McMurdo, S., Watson, T., Mann, C., Gaynor, S., and Mee, L. (2019) 'The Problem of Post-Horror', *In Medias Res*. 4 March–8 March. Available at: http://mediacommons.org/imr/content/problem-post-horror-0 (Accessed: 31/07/2021).

Mee, L. (2017) *The Shining (Devil's Advocates)*. Leighton Buzzard: Auteur.

Mee, L. (2020) 'Murders and Adaptations: Gender in American Psycho', in Peirse, A. (ed.) *Women Make Horror: Feminism, Filmmaking, Genre*. New Brunswick: Rutgers University Press, pp. 91–103.

Mee, L. (2022) *Reanimated: The Contemporary American Horror Remake*. Edinburgh: Edinburgh University Press.

Meisfjord, T. (2019) 'The Pet Sematary Scene That Even Hardened Horror Fans Always Skip', *Looper*. 12 February. Available at: https://www.looper.com/333429/the-pet-sematary-scene-that-even-hardened-horror-fans-always-skip/ (Accessed: 03/07/2021).

Millar, B. and Lee, J. (2021) 'Horror Films and Grief', *Emotion Review*, 13(3), pp. 171–182.

Miller, M. (2016) 'Stranger Things Is Officially Bigger Than *House of Cards* and *Jessica Jones*', *Esquire*. 12 August. Available at: https://www.esquire.com/entertainment/tv/news/a47629/stranger-things-ratings-success/ (Accessed: 03/07/2021).

Mitchell, N. (2013) *Carrie (Devil's Advocates)*. Leighton Buzzard: Auteur.

Morgulis, N. (2019) 'On the Set with Pet Sematary's Producer', *Den of Geek*. 5 April. Available at: https://www.denofgeek.com/movies/on-the-set-with-pet-sematary-s-producer/ (Accessed: 03/07/2021).

Motamayor, R. (2018) '[Editorial] "Hereditary" and the True Horrors of the Grieving Process', *Bloody Disgusting*. 12 June. Available at: https://bloody-disgusting.com/editorials/3503575/hereditary-grieving-times-horror/ (Accessed: 02/07/2021).

Muir, J. K. (2007) *Horror Films of the 1980s*. Jefferson: McFarland and Co.

Mulvey, L. (1975) 'Visual Pleasure and Narrative Cinema', *Screen*, 16(3), pp. 6–18.

Murphy, S. (2017) 'Lonely Graves and the Madness of Despair in "Pet Sematary"', *Medium*. 12 January. Available at: https://medium.com/@shaynamurphy/pet-sematary-lonely-graves-and-the-madness-of-despair-2218e09cb834 (Accessed: 05/08/2021).

Naremore, J. (2000) *Film Adaptation*. New Brunswick: Rutgers University Press.

Nash, J. (1997) 'Post Modern Gothic: Stephen King's Pet Sematary', in Bloom, H. (ed.) *Stephen King*. New York: Chelsea House Publishers, pp. 167–176.

Navarro, M. (2017) 'In Defense of Pet Sematary Two', *Bloody Disgusting*. 28 August. Available at: https://bloody-disgusting.com/editorials/3453663/defense-pet-sematary-two/ (Accessed: 03/08/2021).

Nazare, J. (2000) 'The Horror! The Horror? The Appropriation, and Reclamation, of Native American Mythology', *Journal of the Fantastic in the Arts*, 11(1), pp. 24–51.

Nicoll, G. (1992) 'Two for the Roadkill', *Fangoria*, 117, pp. 46–49.

Nolan, M. (2019) 'The horror of Pet Sematary isn't supernatural – it's the disturbing, ordinary horror of grief', *New Statesman*. 10 April. Available at: https://www.newstatesman.com/culture/books/2019/04/horror-pet-semetary-isn-t-supernatural-it-s-disturbing-ordinary-horror-grief (Accessed: 02/07/2021).

Nutman, P. (1990) 'King Talks', *Fangoria*, 99, pp. 22–26, 59.

Orange, M. (2009) 'Taking Back the Knife: Girls Gone Gory', *The New York Times*. 3 September. Available at: https://www.nytimes.com/2009/09/06/movies/06oran.html (Accessed: 03/07/2021).

Orbey, E. (2016) 'Mourning Through Horror Movies', *New Yorker*. 22 November. Available at: https://www.newyorker.com/books/page-turner/mourning-through-horror-movies (Accessed: 02/07/2021).

O'Quinn, K. (1979) 'Imagination Inc.', *Fangoria*, 1, p. 4.

O'Sullivan, M. (2014) '"Babadook" Director Jennifer Kent Talks About Women Making Horror Movies', *The Washington Post*. 12 December. Available at: https://www.washingtonpost.com/lifestyle/style/babadook-director-jennifer-kent-talks-about-women-making-horror-movies/2014/12/12/11dba89a-8082-11e4-9f38-95a187e4c1f7_story.html (Accessed: 03/07/2021).

Paskiewicz, K. (2017) 'When the Woman Directs (a Horror Film)', in Harrod, M. and Paszkiewicz, K. (eds.) *Women do Genre in Film and Television*. New York: Routledge, pp. 41–56.

Patches, M. (2018) 'Blumhouse Has Never Produced A Theatrically Released Horror Movie Directed By A Woman – But Hopes To', *Polygon*. 18 October. Available at: https://www.polygon.com/2018/10/17/17984162/halloween-blumhouse-female-director (Accessed: 21/07/2021).

Paterson, J. M. R. (2012) 'The Maine Indian Land Claim Settlement: A Personal Recollection', *Maine History*, 46(2), pp. 195–225.

Peirse, A. (2020a) *Women Make Horror: Filmmaking, Feminism, Genre*. New Brunswick: Rutgers University Press.

Peirse, A. (2020b) 'Women Make (Write, Produce, Direct, Shoot, Edit, and Analyze) Horror', in Peirse, A. (ed.) *Women Make Horror: Filmmaking, Feminism, Genre*. New Brunswick: Rutgers University Press, pp. 1–23.

Peoples, G. (1981) 'Blood, Siskel & the Ratings – Postal Zone', *Fangoria*, 10, p. 5.

Pezzotta, E. (2013) *Stanley Kubrick: Adapting the Sublime*. Jackson: University Press of Mississippi.

Pharr, M. F. (1987) 'A Dream of New Life: Stephen King's Pet Sematary as a Variant of Frankenstein', in Hoppenstand, G. and Browne, R. B. (eds.) *The Gothic World of Stephen King: Landscape of Nightmares*. Bowling Green: Bowling Green State University Press, pp. 115–125.

Plante, C. (2019) 'The New "Pet Sematary" Ending Doubles Down On The Demon Invasion Horror', *Inverse*. 5 May. Available at: https://www.inverse.com/article/54645-pet-sematary-2019-ending-explained-spoilers (Accessed: 19/07/2021).

Prince, S. (2002) *A New Pot of Gold: Hollywood Under the Electronic Rainbow, 1980–1989*. Berkeley: University of California Press.

Radcliffe, A. (1826) 'On the Supernatural in Poetry', *New Monthly Magazine*, 16, pp. 145–152.

Raheja, M. (2011) *Reservation Reelism: Redfacing, Visual Sovereignty and Representations of Native Americans in Film*. Nebraska: University of Nebraska Press.

Reyes, X. A. (2020) *Gothic Cinema*. Abingdon: Routledge.

Rose, S. (2017) 'How Post-Horror Movies Are Taking Over Cinema', *The Guardian*. 6 July. Available at: https://www.theguardian.com/film/2017/jul/06/post-horror-films-scary-movies-ghost-story-it-comes-at-night (Accessed: 03/07/2021).

Rossinow, D. (2015) *The Reagan Era: A History of the 1980s*. New York City: Columbia University Press.

Rosza, M. (2019) '"Pet Sematary" Remake Stinks Like A Rotting Corpse', *Salon*. 5 April. Available at: https://www.salon.com/2019/04/05/pet-sematary-remake-stinks-like-a-rotting-corpse/ (Accessed: 03/07/2021).

Savoy, E. (1988) 'The Face of the Tenant: A Theory of American Gothic', in Martin, R. K. and Savoy, E. (eds.) *American Gothic: New Interventions in a National Narrative*. Iowa City: University of Iowa Press, pp. 3–19.

Schroeder, N. (1987) '"Oz the Gweat and Tewwible" and "The Other Side": The Theme of Death in Pet Sematary and Jitterbug Perfume', in Hoppenstand, G. and Browne, R. B. (eds.) *The Gothic World of Stephen King: Landscape of Nightmares*. Bowling Green: Bowling Green State University Press, pp. 135–141.

Schulman, B. J. (2001) *The Seventies: A Great Shift in American Culture, Society and Politics*. New York: Free Press.

Schuman, S. (1987) 'Taking Stephen King Seriously: Reflections on a Decade of Best-Sellers', in Hoppenstand, G. and Browne, R. B. (eds.) *The Gothic World of Stephen King: Landscape of Nightmares*. Bowling Green: Bowling Green State University Press, pp. 107–114.

Sears, J. (2011) *Stephen King's Gothic*. Cardiff: University of Wales Press.

Shapiro, M. (1993) 'Monster Invasion', *Fangoria*, 49, p. 10.

Sharrett, C. (1993) 'The Horror Film in Neoconservative Culture', *Journal of Popular Film and Television*, 21(3), pp. 100–110.

Siskel, G. (1989) '"84 Charlie Mopic" Takes You On Patrol in Vietnam', *The Chicago Tribune*. 28 April. Available at: https://www.chicagotribune.com/news/ct-xpm-1989-04-28-8904080211-story.html (Accessed: 08/08/2021).

Snelson, T. (2014) *Phantom Ladies: Hollywood Horror and the Home Front*. New Brunswick: Rutgers University Press.

Sobchack, V. (1987) 'Bringing It All Back Home: Family Economy and Generic Exchange', reprinted in Grant, B. K. (ed.) (2015) *The Dread of Difference: Gender and The Horror Film*. Austin: University of Texas Press, pp. 171–191.

Sobczynski, P. (2019) 'Pet Sematary', *Roger Ebert*. 5 April. Available at: https://www.rogerebert.com/reviews/pet-sematary-2019 (Accessed: 21/07/2021).

Squires, J. (2021) 'Lindsay Beer Directing New "Pet Sematary" Movie for Paramount; May or May Not Be a Prequel Tale', *Bloody Disgusting*. 17 May. Available at: https://bloody-disgusting.com/movie/3665550/lindsey-beer-directing-new-pet-sematary-movie-paramount-may-may-not-prequel-tale/ (Accessed: 30/03/2022).

Strengell, H. (2005) 'The Ghost: the Gothic Melodrama in Stephen King's Fiction', *European Journal of American Culture*, 24(3), pp. 221–238.

Strick, P. (1989) 'Pet Sematary', *The Monthly Film Bulletin*, 56, p. 342.

Stroby, W. (1992) 'King on a Roll', *Fangoria*, 113, pp. 26–31.

Szebin, F. (1989a) 'Pet Sematary: Stephen King's Horror Bestseller Gets Filmed the Way He Wants', *Cinefantastique*, 19(3), pp. 4–6.

Szebin, F. (1989b) 'Mary Lambert on Directing Stephen King's Pet Sematary', *Cinefantastique*, 20(1–2), pp. 122–123.

Tafoya, S. (2019) 'The Pain Needs to Mean Something: On Horror and Grief', *Roger Ebert*. 26 August. Available at: https://www.rogerebert.com/features/the-pain-needs-to-mean-something-on-horror-and-grief (Accessed: 02/07/2021).

Tangcay, J. (2020) '"Pet Sematary" Director Mary Lambert on Using Old-Fashioned Effects for Scares in Pre-CGI Stephen King Adaptation', *Variety*. 16 October. Available at: https://variety.com/2020/artisans/production/pet-sematary-director-mary-lambert-1234806633/ (Accessed: 30/03/2022).

Taylor, T. (2020) 'Self-Reflexivity and Feminist Camp in Freddy's Dead: The Final Nightmare', in Peirse, A. (ed.) *Women Make Horror: Feminism, Filmmaking, Genre*. New Brunswick: Rutgers University Press, pp. 69–80.

Thompson, S. (2019) 'Stephen King, Denny's And The Dead: Mary Lambert Talks "Pet Sematary" 30 Years On', *Forbes*. 4 April. Available at: https://www.forbes.com/sites/simonthompson/2019/04/04/stephen-king-dennys-and-the-dead-mary-lambert-talks-pet-sematary-30-years-on/?sh=56c89e4a4c6e (Accessed: 04/08/2021).

Timpone, T. (1988) 'Monster Invasion', *Fangoria*, 76, p. 11.

Timpone, T. (1991) 'Elegy', *Fangoria*, 102, p. 6.

Timpone, T. (2005) 'Dead Pet Misery', *Fangoria*, 239, p. 66–69, 82.

Tompkins, J. (2014) 'Bids for Distinction: The Critical-Industrial function of the Horror Auteur', in Nowell, R. (ed.) *Merchants of Menace: The Business of Horror Cinema*. London: Bloomsbury Academic, pp. 203–214.

Towlson, J. (2014) *Subversive Horror Cinema: Countercultural Messages of Films from Frankenstein to the Present*. Jefferson: McFarland and Co.

Trecansky, S. (2001) 'Final Girls and Terrible Youth: Transgression in 1980s Slasher Horror', *Journal of Popular Film and Television*, 29(2), pp. 63–73.

Troy, G. (2005) *Morning in America: How Ronald Reagan Invented the 1980s*. Princeton: Princeton University Press.

Tyler, L. (2019) 'Why I Love Horror Movies', *Medium*. August 7. Available at: https://medium.com/@lila_t/why-i-love-horror-movies-90f119fd5c46 (Accessed: 23/11/2022).

Valenti, L. (2020) 'Who Will Win Best Hair and Makeup at the Oscars 2020? The Past Has Some Clues', *Variety*. 15 January. Available at: https://www.vogue.com/slideshow/academy-award-for-best-makeup-and-hairstyling (Accessed: 25/06/2021).

Variety Staff (1985) 'Maximum Overdrive', *Variety*. 31 December. Available at: https://variety.com/1985/film/reviews/maximum-overdrive-1200426863/ (Accessed: 25/06/2021).

Variety Staff (1989) 'Pet Sematary', *Variety*. 31 December. Available at: https://variety.com/1988/film/reviews/pet-sematary-1200427883/ (Accessed: 08/08/2021).

Varma, D. (1966) *The Gothic Flame*. New York: Russell and Russell.

Vespe, E. (2019) 'Pet Sematary Directors Reveal Stephen King Easter Eggs and Talk About That Big Change', *Syfy*. 19 March. https://www.syfy.com/syfywire/pet-sematary-directors-reveal-stephen-king-easter-eggs-and-talk-about-that-big-change (Accessed: 04/08/2021; no longer available).

Waller, G. (1987) 'Introduction', in Waller, G. (ed.) *American Horror: Essays on the Modern American Horror Film*. Champaign: University of Illinois Press, pp. 1–13.

Wang, E. (2017) 'Welcome to the Golden Age of Women-Directed Horror', *Vice*. 14 April. Available at: https://www.vice.com/en/article/zmbnd5/welcome-to-the-golden-age-of-women-directed-horror (Accessed: 04/08/2021).

Webster, L. (2022) '"Scary Monsters (and Super Creeps)": Critiquing Representations of Women Throughout the 1980s in *Fangoria* Magazine', *Horror Studies*, 13, pp. 209–229.

Webster, P. (2011) *Love and Death in Kubrick: A Critical Study of the Films from* Lolita *through* Eyes Wide Shut. Jefferson: McFarland and Co.

Weiner, D. (2019) 'How Original "Pet Sematary" Director Won Over Stephen King', *Hollywood Reporter*. 29 March. Available at: https://www.hollywoodreporter.com/movies/movie-features/how-pet-sematary-director-won-stephen-king-1198107/ (Accessed: 03/07/2021).

Weinstock, J. A. (2008) 'Maybe It Shouldn't Be a Party: Kids, Keds, and Death in Stephen King's *Stand By Me* and *Pet Sematary*', in Magistrale, T. (ed.) *The Films of Stephen King*. New York: Palgrave MacMillan, pp. 39–49.

Weiss, J. (2019) 'A Lesson In Adaptation: Why We Were Deathly Wrong To Worry Over That Big Change In "Pet Sematary"', *Forbes*. 5 April. Available at: https://www.forbes.com/sites/joshweiss/2019/04/05/a-lesson-in-adaptation-why-we-were-deathly-wrong-to-worry-over-that-big-change-up-in-pet-sematary/?sh=51ab021b2cb4 (Accessed: 19/07/2021).

Williams, L. (1983) 'When the Woman Looks', reprinted in Grant, B. K. (ed.) (2015) *The Dread of Difference: Gender and The Horror Film*. Austin: University of Texas Press, pp. 17–36.

Williams, O. (2013) 'Fango Unchained', *Empire* 286, pp. 110–117.

Williams, T. (2015) 'Trying to Survive on the Darker Side: 1980s Family Horror', in Grant, B. K. (ed.) *The Dread of Difference: Gender and the Horror Film*. Austin: University of Texas Press, pp. 192–208.

Wilson, E. (2003) *Cinema's Missing Children*. London: Wallflower Press.

Wingrove, N. and Morris, M. (2009) *Art of the Nasty*. Surrey: FAB Press.

Winkelman, S. (1992) 'No Femmes in Fame? Shame! – Postal Zone', *Fangoria*, 117, p. 9.

Winter, D. A. (1982) *Stephen King, Starmont Readers Guide*. Mercer Island: Starmont House.

Winter, D. A. (1989) *The Art of Darkness: The Life and Fiction of the Master of the Macabre, Stephen King*. London: New English Library.

Wojnar, Z. (2019) 'Mary Lambert Interview: Pet Sematary 30th Anniversary', *Screen Rant*. 28 March. Available at: https://screenrant.com/pet-sematary-mary-lambert-interview/ (Accessed: 14/07/2021).

Wollenberg, S. (1989) 'Pepsi Drops Ads with Madonna', *AP News*. 4 April. Available at: https://apnews.com/article/fd42ea3ca314eb0741027e186acdb5e5 (Accessed: 07/07/2021).

Wood, G. (1991) 'Pet Sematary', *Cinefantastique*, 21(4), p. 39.

Wood, R. (1979) *American Nightmare: Essays on the Horror Film*. Toronto: Festival of Festivals.

Wood, R. (2003) *Hollywood from Vietnam to Reagan… and Beyond*. New York: Columbia University Press.

Wood, R. (2004) 'Foreword: "What Lies Beneath"', in Schneider, S. J. (ed.) *Horror Film and Psychoanalysis: Freud's Worst Nightmare*. Cambridge: Cambridge University Press, pp. xiii–xviii.

Yamato, J. (2019) 'Q&A: Original "Pet Sematary" director Mary Lambert on Madonna and Stephen King Meetings at Denny's', *Los Angeles Times*. 4 April. Available at: https://www.latimes.com/entertainment/movies/la-et-mn-pet-sematary-mary-lambert-director-stephen-king-madonna-20190404-story.html (Accessed: 03/07/2021).

www.ingramcontent.com/pod-product-compliance
Lightning Source LLC
Chambersburg PA
CBHW070403240426
43661CB00056B/2522